Color Mixing Recipes

FOR PORTRAITS

More Than 500 Color Combinations for Skin, Eyes, Lips, and Hair

BY WILLIAM F. POWELL

Quarto.com • WalterFoster.com

First Published in 2006 by Walter Foster Publishing, an imprint of The Quarto Group.
100 Cummings Center, Suite 265D, Beverly, MA 01915, USA.
T (978) 282-9590 **F** (978) 283-2742

EEA Representation, WTS Tax d.o.o.,
Žanova ulica 3, 4000 Kranj, Slovenia.
www.wts-tax.si

Walter Foster Publishing titles are also available at discount for retail, wholesale, promotional, and bulk purchase. For details, contact the Special Sales Manager by email at specialsales@quarto.com or by mail at The Quarto Group, Attn: Special Sales Manager, 100 Cummings Center, Suite 265D, Beverly, MA 01915, USA.

ISBN: 978-1-56010-990-7

Printed in Guangdong, China TT122025
30 29

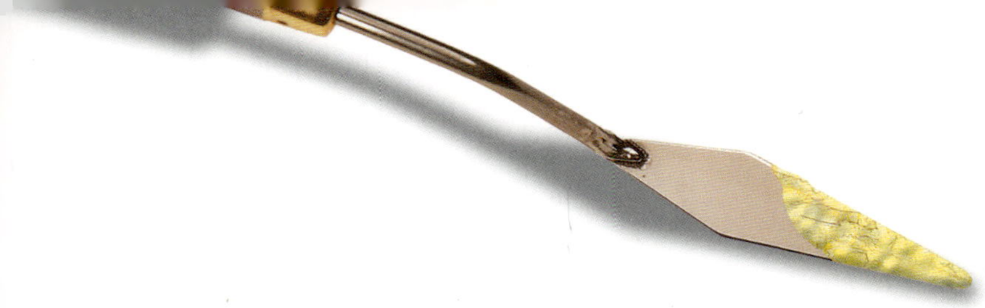

Contents

INTRODUCTION

This book features harmonious mixes for 24 specific skin tones, from the dominant color to its range of values, shadows, and highlights. Each skin tone palette will help you achieve color unity in your portraits. You can paint an entire portrait using only the recipes shown with each skin tone palette or you can intermix palettes to create new recipes (see examples on pages 44–45).

MEASURING OIL AND ACRYLIC COLORS

Begin by removing the plastic Color Mixing Grid from the back of this book and selecting a skin tone recipe. Then squeeze out the colors on your grid according to the recipe, using each square as one part. (All oil and acrylic recipes use a "part" as the basic unit of measurement.) Be sure to squeeze out the paint in uniform widths and lengths for each part to keep the proportions consistent. Sometimes only a very small amount of color is needed in a recipe; in this case, the amount is referred to as a "speck" and is equal to about the size of a large pinhead.

MEASURING WATERCOLOR COLORS

On pages 38–43, you'll find a section on mixing watercolor. This process involves percentages rather than parts, so you may want to create a special grid. (See bottom photo and caption for instructions.) With watercolor, the ratio of paint to water is just as important as the paint proportions. To help you achieve the correct level of dilution for each recipe, follow the color intensity guidelines (level 1–level 4). Level 1 is a pale color and requires the most amount of water, whereas level 2 is still weak in color but uses a bit less water than level 1. Level 3 is a medium color (again using a bit less water), whereas level 4 is a strong color using very little water. Level 5 requires no water and is used only when creating Master Skin Tone Recipes.

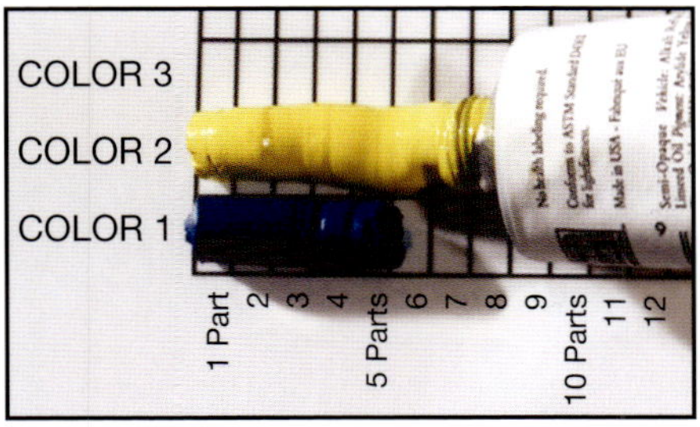

▲ **USING THE COLOR MIXING GRID** You can use the color mixing grid to measure paint for your mixes. When making your own mixes, note the quantity of each color for future reference.

Tip: Keep your mixtures simple. Don't mix too many different colors together because the color may become "muddy." However, even muddy colors can be beautiful when used properly.

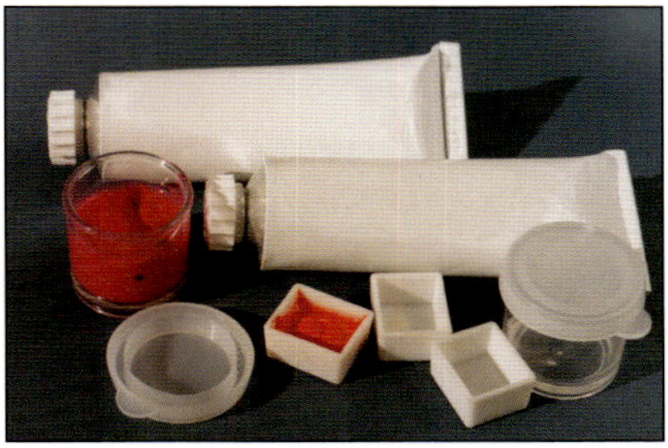

▲ **MIXING AND STORING LARGE AMOUNTS OF COLOR** You can mix and store large amounts of a mixed color for future use. Once mixed, color can be stored in empty containers made for this purpose. For oil and acrylic, you can purchase empty paint tubes and label your own colors. For watercolor, purchase inexpensive empty pans or tiny plastic containers with lids.

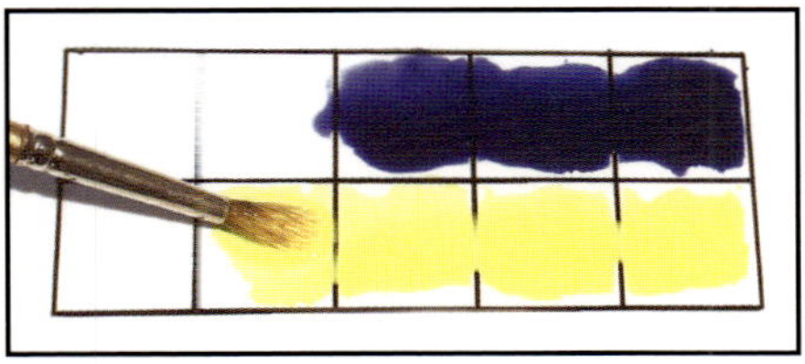

◀ **MAKING AND USING A WATERCOLOR GRID** Using a permanent marker, draw two rows of five adjoining one-inch squares on a palette or a piece of glass or plastic. Wet your brush and pull color onto the squares in the suggested ratio. (Each square represents 10%.) Mix the colors in their listed order until you achieve the desired color.

PURCHASING COLORS

There are hundreds of skin tones around the world, and this book contains recipes for a comprehensive range of them. (You'll even discover methods for creating more variations.) You will need to purchase the colors listed on the inside front cover of this book to re-create all the palettes.

SkinTonePalettes BASIC MIXES

Yellow ochre is the most common color used in basic skin tone palettes. The samples below show yellow ochre mixed with different reds. First create a master recipe to the desired yellow or red tone. The recipe can be lightened, darkened, grayed, or intermixed.

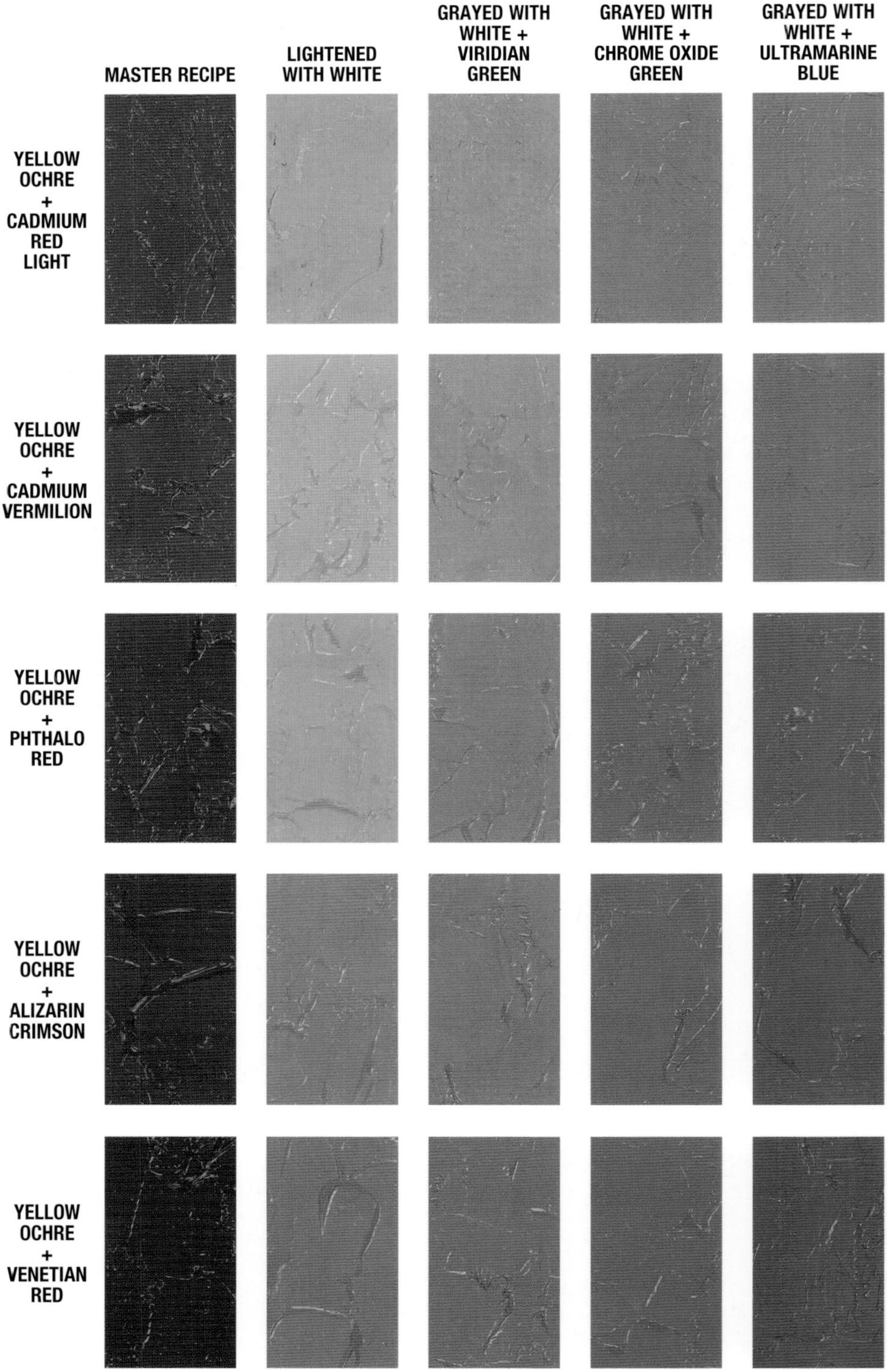

SkinTonePalettes BASIC MIXES

Naples yellow hue is a light, warm yellow that also mixes well with reds for skin tone palettes. The samples below show Naples yellow hue mixed with different reds. First create a master recipe to the desired yellow or red tone. The recipe can be lightened, darkened, grayed, or intermixed.

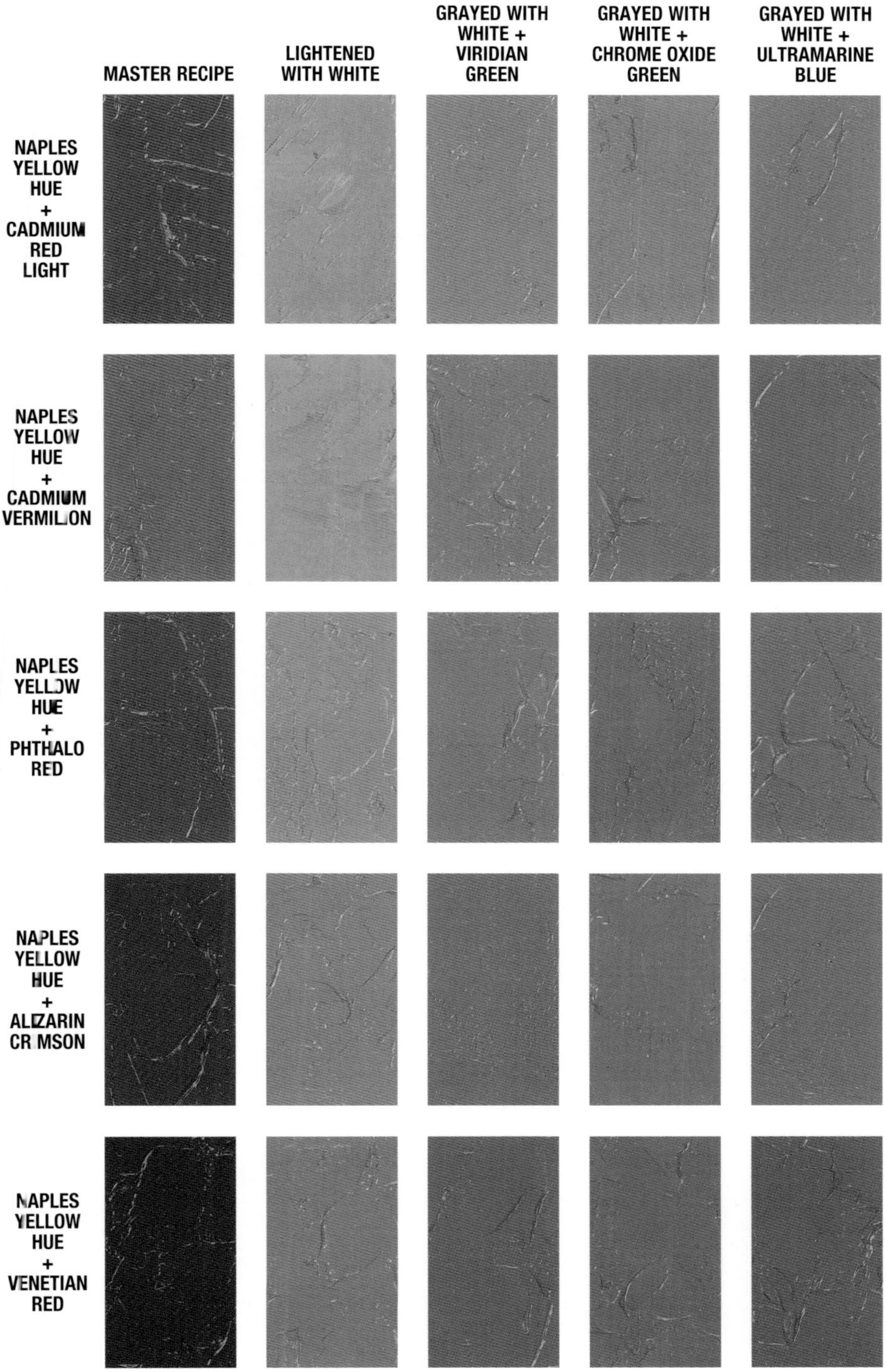

ColorTheory TINTING, TONING & SHADING

Value refers to the lightness or darkness of a color or a tone. On a value scale of white to black, white represents light and black represents darkness, which is the absence of light and therefore the absence of color.

Adding white to a color results in a **tint** of that color.
Adding gray to a color results in a **tone** of that color.
Adding black to a color results in a **shade** of that color.

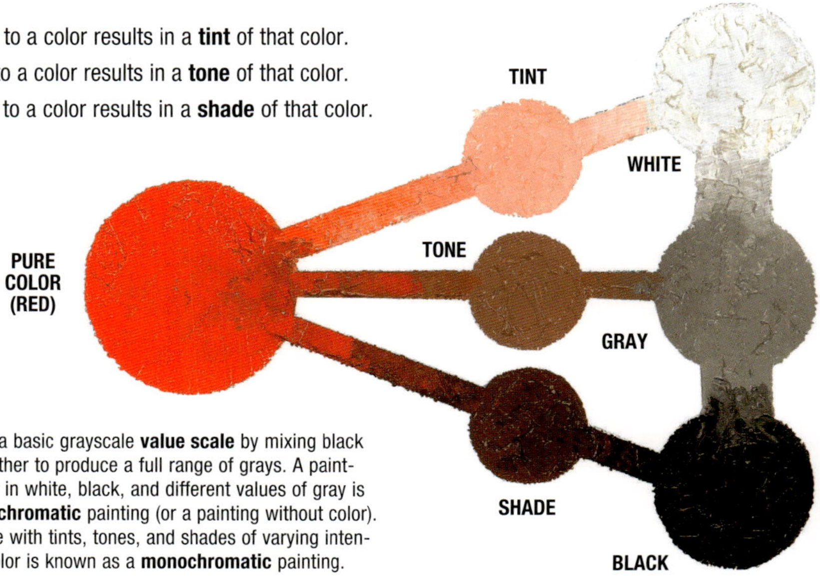

You can make a basic grayscale **value scale** by mixing black and white together to produce a full range of grays. A painting done solely in white, black, and different values of gray is known as an **achromatic** painting (or a painting without color). A painting done with tints, tones, and shades of varying intensities of one color is known as a **monochromatic** painting.

KEEPING SKIN TONE MIXES LIVELY WHEN TINTING AND SHADING

Keep color mixes "fresh" by following the two simple rules shown below.

When you add white to a color, simply add a touch of the color **above** it on the color wheel to keep the lighter mixture fresh.

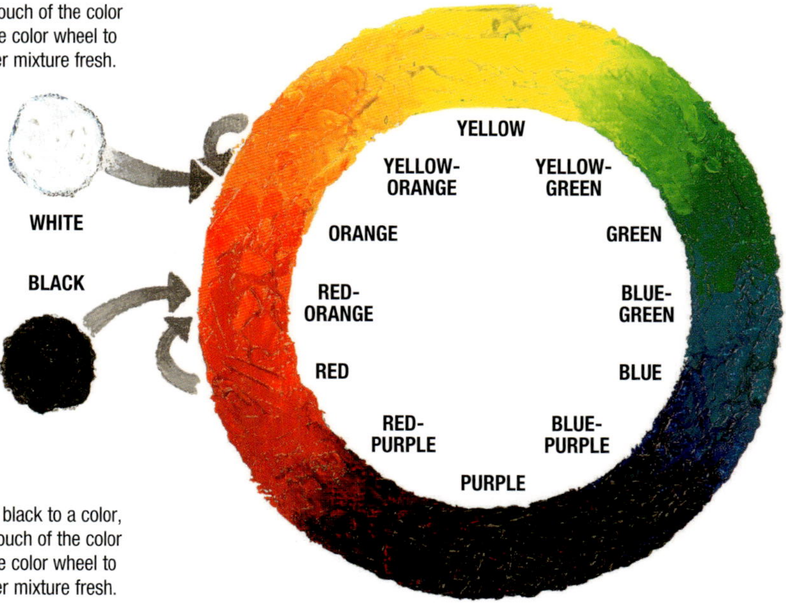

When you add black to a color, simply add a touch of the color **below** it on the color wheel to keep the darker mixture fresh.

When adding white or black to a color, the extra color selected from either above or below the color should be close to the original color on the wheel. If you choose a color that is too far away, you will make a new color. The two colors should be analogous. (Colors that resemble one another but are slightly different and are close to one another on the color wheel are **analogous** colors.)

ColorTheory GRAYING SKIN TONES NATURALLY

As shown on page 6, a color cannot be "grayed" using black or white—it can be only tinted, toned, or shaded.

Colors directly across the color wheel from each another, such as red and green, are known as "direct complements." Direct complements have the ability to neutralize or "gray" each other. When you mix two direct complementary colors, the result is a natural, neutral color. The mixture at right shows yellow ochre and cadmium vermilion mixed for a skin tone that can be grayed with viridian green (vermilion's complement) or tinted with white.

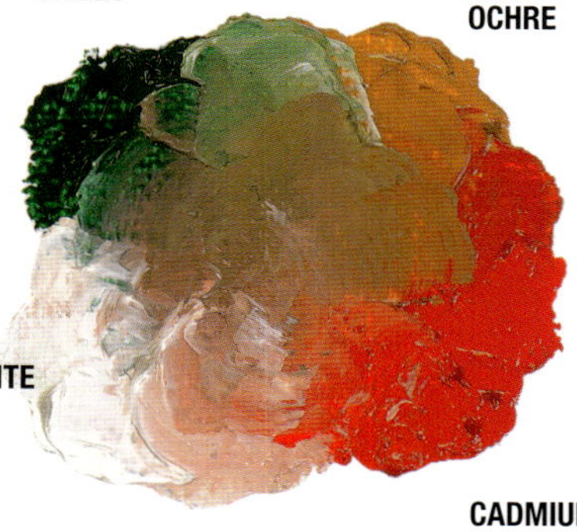

As you mix skin tones, it's a good idea to make test "smearings" to find the best mixtures. The sample at left shows cerulean blue hue mixed with viridian green and white, producing a soft blue-green. Combining these with the skin tone recipe of Naples yellow hue and cadmium red light yields a beautiful, natural gray of each.

This example shows two colors (cadmium red light and cerulean blue hue) that have been tinted with white. Even though these colors are tinted, they still remain complementary to each other. Notice the beautiful grayed color in the center created by mixing the two colors.

Here you see a light, cool blue (ultramarine) mixed with a warm reddish-orange mix of burnt sienna and cadmium vermilion. Orange and blue are direct complements, so they gray each other well. Notice the graduations of grayed colors in the center of this sample.

BASIC PALETTES

If your model's skin color doesn't match any palettes in this book, you can use the color mixes on the next two pages as a base for mixing the exact tone you need. Start with any mix and lighten, darken, or gray as indicated below until you achieve the desired color.

To Lighten Add other, lighter skin tones, or try adding white to colors like zinc yellow, cadmium yellow light, Naples yellow hue, or cadmium orange.

To Darken Add other, darker skin tones, or try adding burnt umber, burnt sienna, alizarin crimson, ultramarine blue, or mixtures of the above colors. To shade a tone, add a touch of black.

To Gray Add one or more of the following colors: white plus ultramarine blue, chrome oxide green, cadmium yellow light, cerulean blue hue, or cadmium orange. Also add a complementary color: If the tone is red, add green; if yellow, add purple.

1. Medium Mix

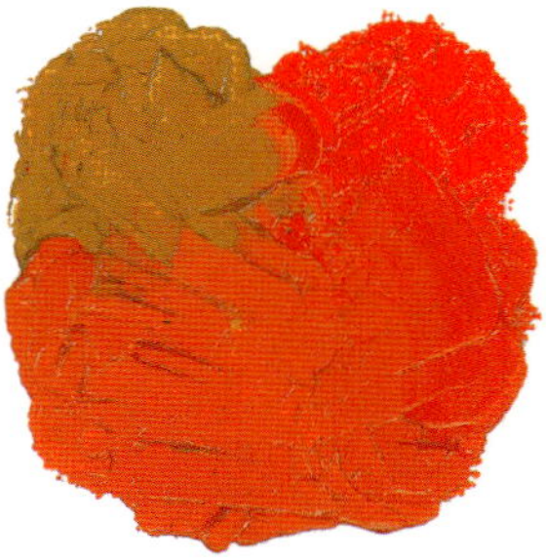

YELLOW OCHRE + CADMIUM RED LIGHT

2. Light Mix

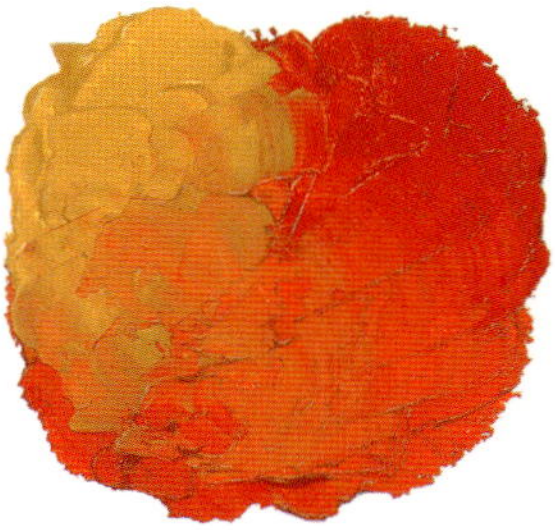

NAPLES YELLOW HUE + CADMIUM RED LIGHT

3. Ruddy Mix

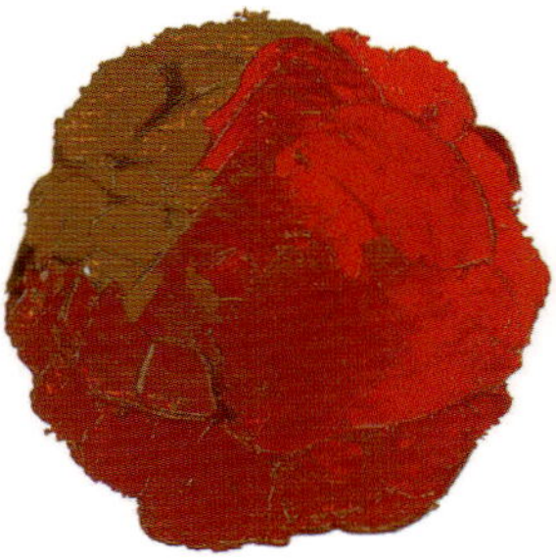

BURNT SIENNA + CADMIUM RED LIGHT

4. Medium-Dark Mix

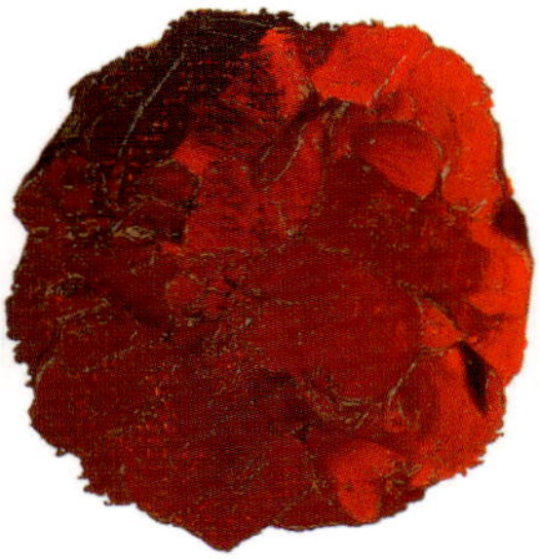

RAW SIENNA + CADMIUM VERMILION

5. Dark Mix

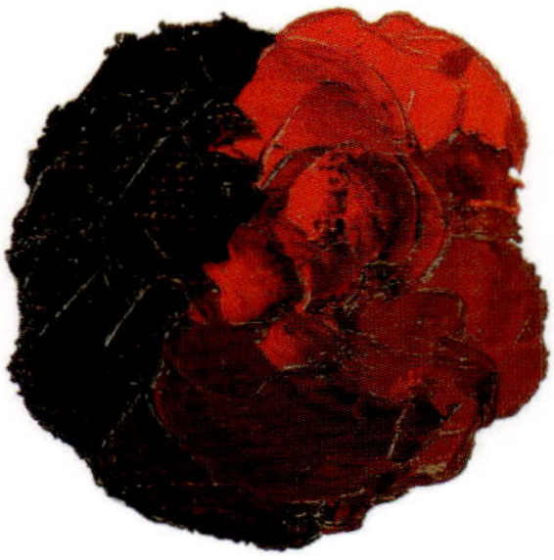

BURNT UMBER + CADMIUM VERMILION

MODIFYING COLORS

The two mixtures at right, **modifying colors,** can be used tone down light flesh colors, to deepen and bronze reddish colors, and to warm or cool shadow colors.

1. Cool Purple Mix

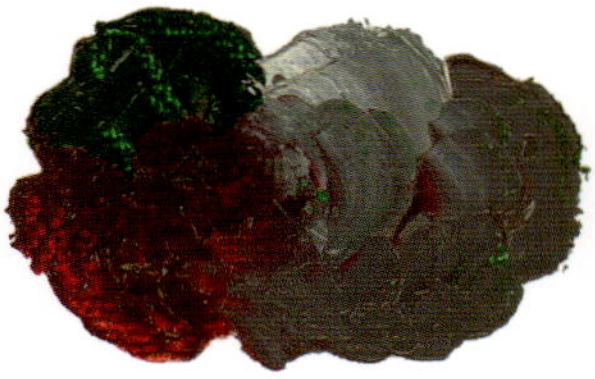

ALIZARIN CRIMSON + VIRIDIAN GREEN + WHITE

2. Warm Purple Mix

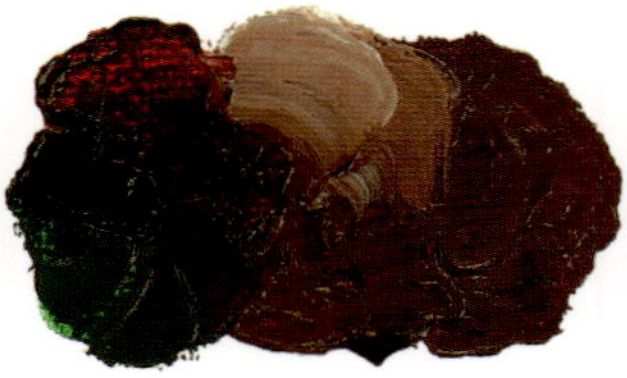

ALIZARIN CRIMSON + WHITE + BURNT UMBER + VIRIDIAN GREEN

FAIR SKIN TONES

The combination of colors below can be used as a base for fair skin tones. You can create many skin tones using this palette. Phthalo red is the key color here—mix it with white to produce pink, or add white and the other colors shown to change the value. Gray or warm the mixes to create soft and light flesh tones. Try to keep the colors delicate and not too harsh or pure. Play with these colors first, and then develop some original palettes. (Note: When painting a flesh color, never use any red in its pure state.)

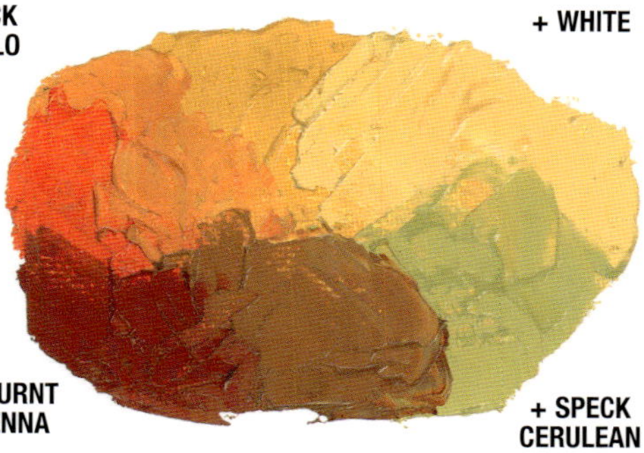

BURNT UMBER TO BRONZE

The palette at right is a base for skin tones that range in hue from burnt umber to bronze. Manipulate the colors to create a wide variety of skin tones. Note that some skin tones have a rich, warm undertone; others are delicately cool. Also take note of subtle colors that can appear under various lighting; look for delicate colors in the shadows and lively tints in the light areas. Depending on the model, shadows can be warm, cool, or even purple or green.

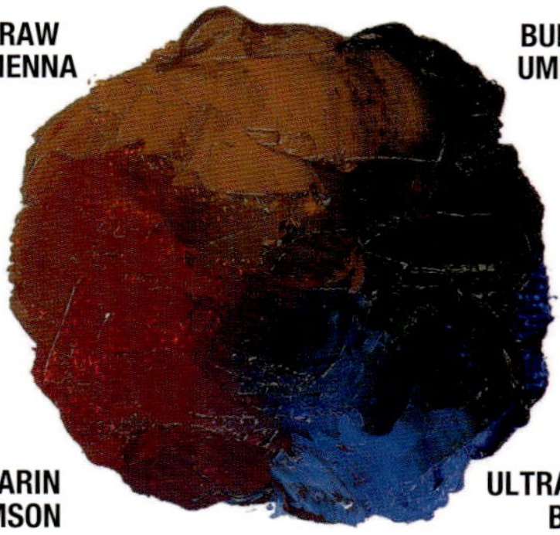

LIGHT BRONZE TO YELLOW OCHRE

You can use this palette as a base for skin tones that range in hue from light bronze to yellow ochre. The more burnt sienna and red in the mix, the more bronze the color will be. Adding more yellow ochre moves the mix toward lighter tones. You can lighten these mixes with a bit of white, but be careful when adding white to darker tones, as it can make them appear milky. Adding a speck of Venetian red will warm the colors. Experiment and remember that these introductory colors can lead to an endless number of skin tone palettes.

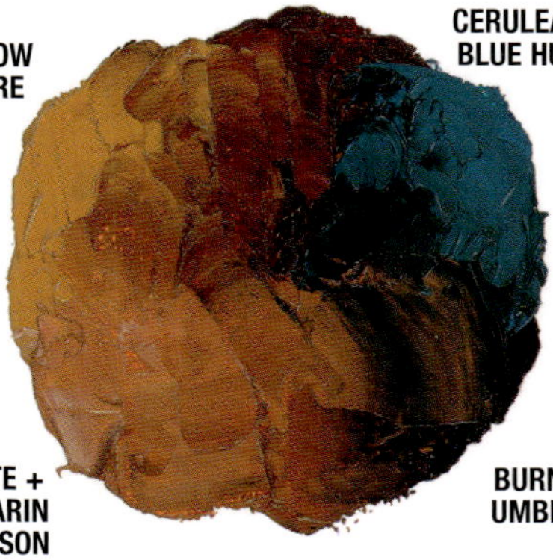

ColorTheory FACIAL PLANES

Variations in value create form and the illusion of depth, so it's important to learn to control these values. Comparing tonal values of black and white to color tones is a helpful exercise. Start with pure white and pure black at the two ends of your value scale; then mix the sample values at right in the following order to obtain a smooth graduation: 9, 8, 6, 7, 5, 4, 2, and 3.

TONAL VALUES

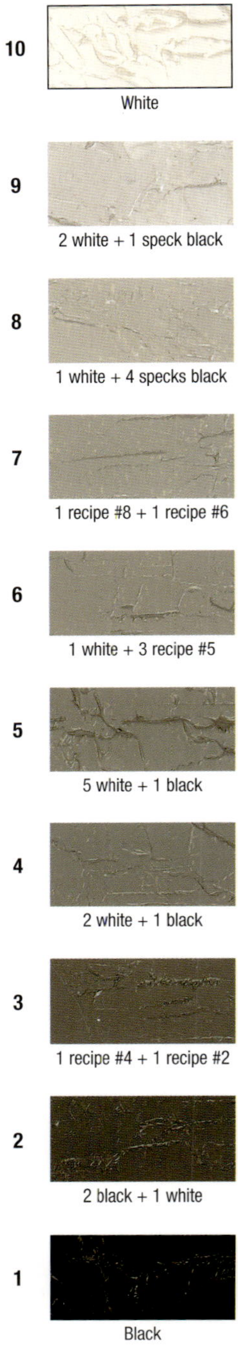

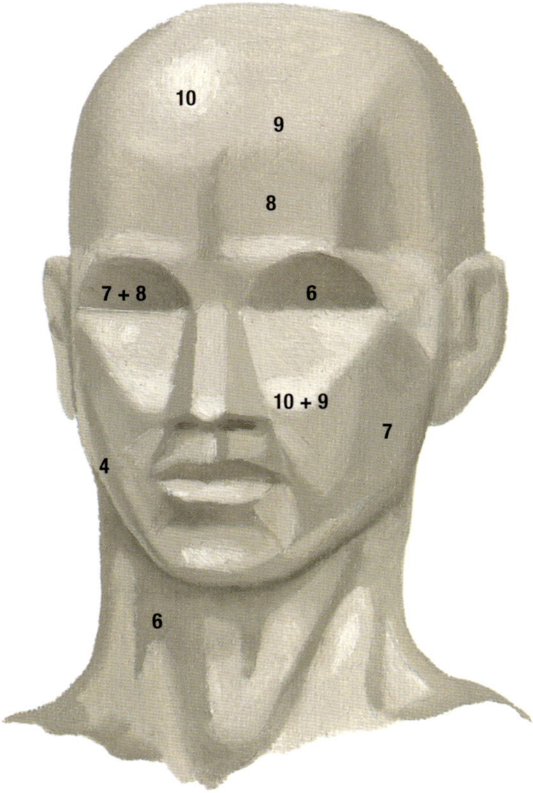

The samples below show how changes in tone create the illusion of depth. The square is blended and the sphere is segmented.

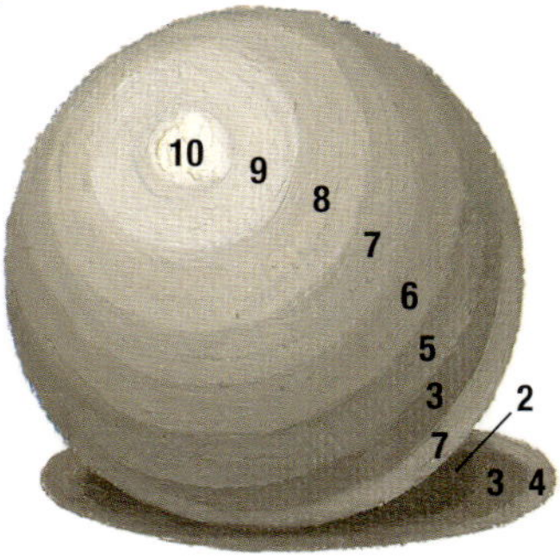

I use a value scale based on the Munsell Value System, with 10 representing white (or "light," a combination of all colors created by light), graduating to 1, or black (the absence of light and color). Some artists reverse these numbers. I painted the head study above from an artist's wooden mannequin; I have placed a few references on it as a visual guide to the scale.

COLOR VALUES

Seeing the value of colors is crucial to creating realistic forms. Tonal value scales, like the one on page 10, also are wonderful guides for comparing color values. For your reference, the colors in this scale are numbered to match their corresponding gray values on the other scale. The colors featured on this page are from the palette on page 14.

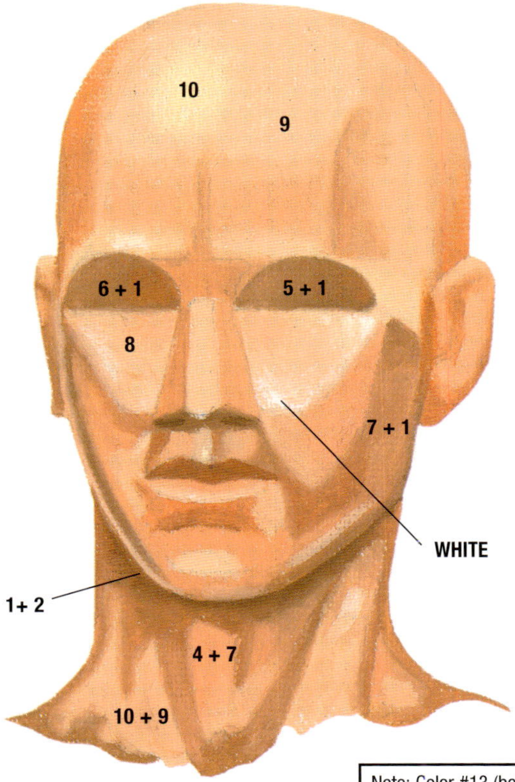

The samples below show how changes in value create the illusion of depth. The square is blended and the sphere is segmented.

Note: Color #13 (below) refers to the cool shadow color on page 14.

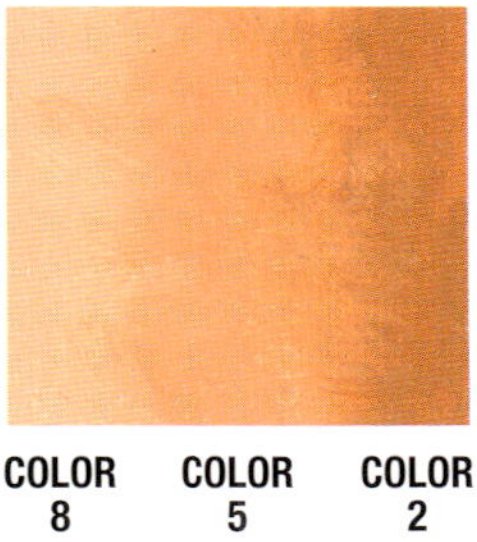

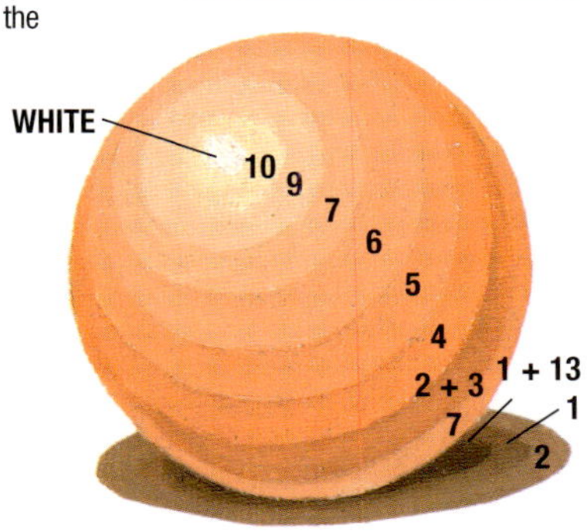

Notice that the color value number placements on this head study vary slightly from the grayscale study on page 10. This is because different skin tone palettes vary in value and tone from warm and cool to creamy and bronze. Due to these differences, use the value scale as a reference, not an absolute. Some palettes may relate only to limited portions of the scale; nonetheless, the scale is a great guide for color tone control. Study each palette and relate each color to a value on the scale.

MouthColorTones

WARM AND COOL AREAS IN AND AROUND THE MOUTH

The skin is thinner on the mouth and blood is closer to the surface, making this area redder than other areas of skin. At times, areas in and around the mouth can appear to be warmer than the rest of the face, as weather and emotions can flush the lips. The upper lip is usually more shadowed than the lower lip, and it casts a shadow on the top of the lower lip. The mixtures shown on this page work as ideal basic lip color mixes that can be darkened, lightened, or grayed, depending on the model.

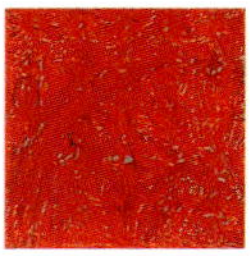

1. Warming Color
3 yellow ochre +
2 cadmium red light +
1 speck alizarin crimson

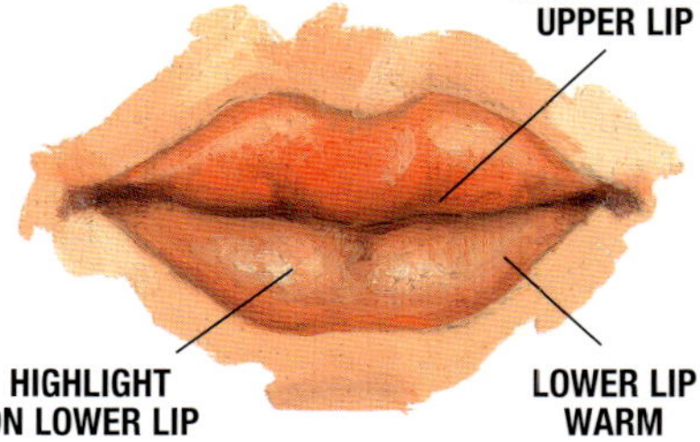

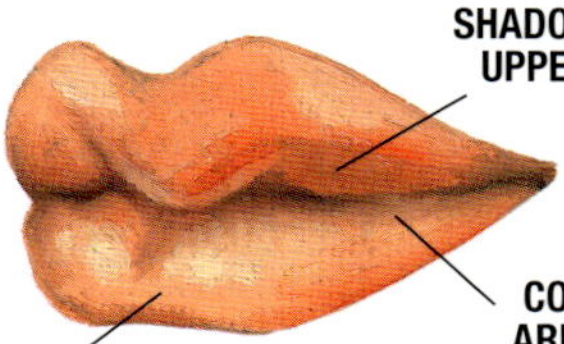

Add Venetian red and white to soften the lip colors where needed. Keep highlights soft to prevent the lips from appearing shiny. The highlight on the lower lip should be the lightest light.

2. Warm Shadow
1 burnt umber +
1 alizarin crimson +
1 cadmium red light

Alter these mixes using a master skin tone recipe plus white, burnt sienna, Naples yellow hue, and cobalt blue; add Venetian red and burnt umber to deepen.

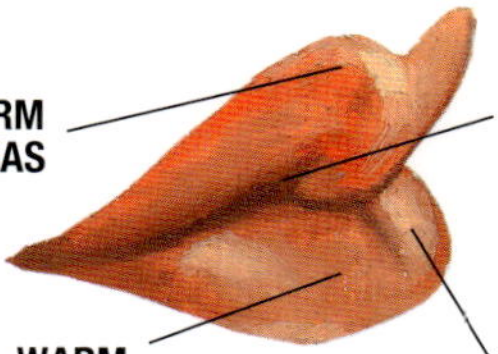

3. Cool Shadow
2 alizarin crimson +
1 ultramarine blue

4. Lightening Color
2 white +
1 speck Naples yellow hue

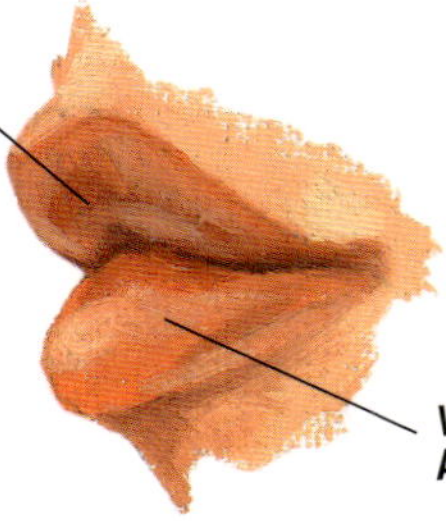

Varying edge lines adds life to the mouth. Some lines are soft and "lost," whereas others are hard and definite. Use alizarin crimson and burnt umber for the deep shadows at the corners. Add specks of ultramarine blue and alizarin crimson for cooler purple shadows. For lower lip highlights, use a pale pink with the lightening color and different reds. White plus Venetian red makes a nice natural pink. The lightening color plus any pink can make an effective lip highlight. White plus alizarin crimson makes a cool pink, whereas white plus a speck of cadmium red light creates a warm pink. Remember to keep all value changes subtle for a realistic look.

WARM AND COOL AREAS IN AND AROUND THE EARS AND NOSE

Many delicate color changes can take place in the creases and curves of the ears and nose. The tops of the ears can become red with the flow of blood, whereas the nose can become red at the tip. The following basic mixes can be deepened or lightened, depending on the model.

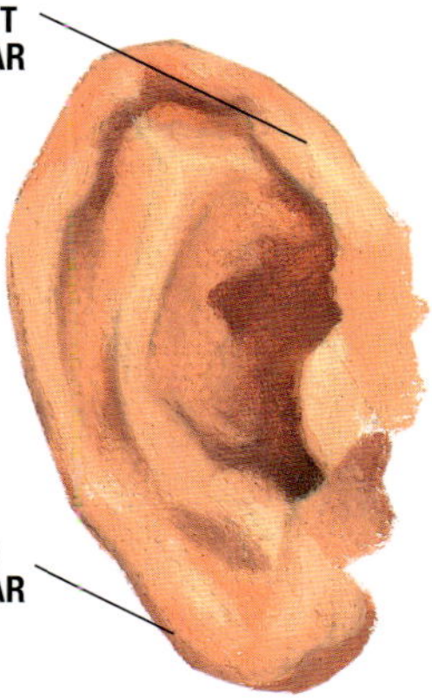

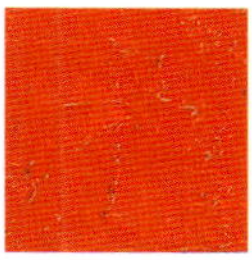

1. Warming Color
3 yellow ochre +
2 cadmium red light

2. Warm Shadow
3 yellow ochre +
1 recipe #1 +
1 alizarin crimson

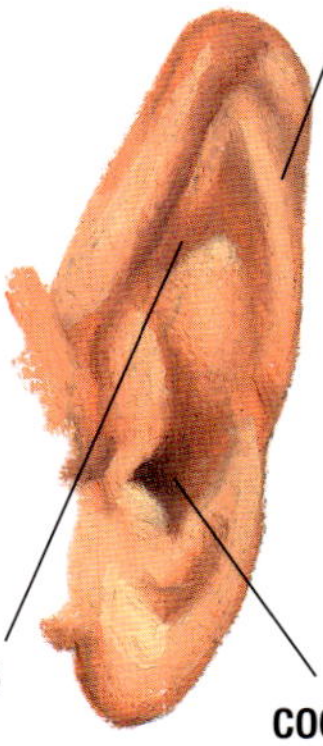

Colors selected for these warmer areas should be muted in intensity. Cadmium red light is very bright if used too strongly. Cadmium vermilion and Venetian red are more muted and will tone down the color. If shadow colors become too strong, gray them with a speck of burnt umber, ultramarine blue, viridian green, or chrome oxide green. As with the mouth, use a variety of reds for different tones. Keep purple mixes for the shadows delicate and not too strong—or they will give a bruised appearance. Colors used in the mouth, ears, and nose must be harmonious with the flesh tone of the subject. Simply use these basic mixes to manipulate the overall skin tones.

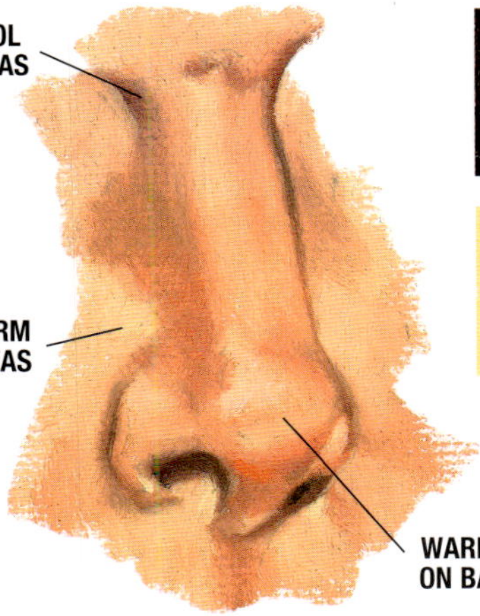

3. Cool Shadow
1 burnt umber +
2 alizarin crimson

4. Lightening Color
1 white +
1 speck Naples
yellow hue

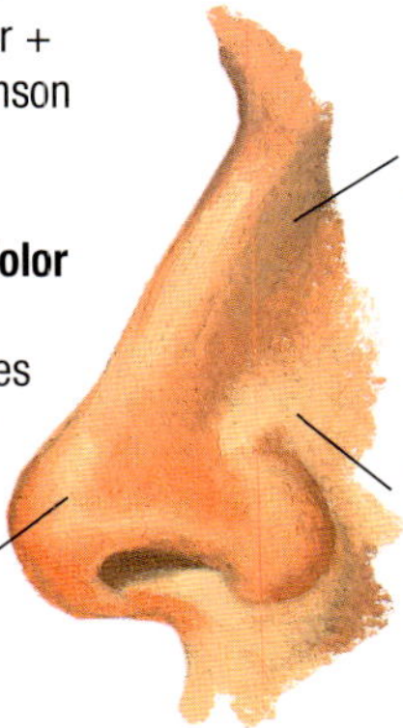

The placement of the mouth, eyes, nose, and ears in relationship to one another on the cranial mass is of the utmost importance. Even the slightest variation of a feature's position can change the expression of the portrait. Any slight misplacement will also change the features of the subject enough to lose the likeness. Study the subject closely and take note of even the subtlest tone changes in the flesh of the ears, nose, and mouth.

SkinToneRecipes

COLORS USED

- Burnt Sienna
- Cadmium Red Light
- Ivory Black
- Naples Yellow Hue
- Raw Umber
- Titanium White
- Viridian Green
- Yellow Ochre

Mix until the color matches the **Master Skin Tone Recipe** shown at right.

1. 3 cadmium red light
2 yellow ochre

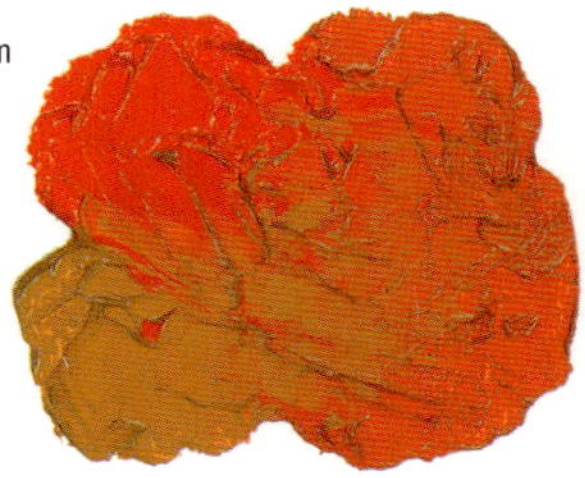

MASTER SKIN TONE RECIPE

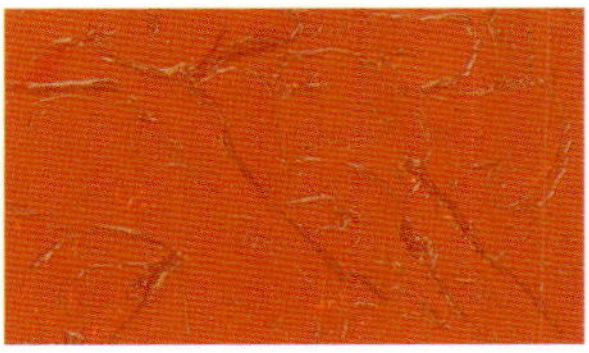

LIGHT VALUES

2. 2 white
1 speck master recipe
1 speck Naples yellow hue

3. 1 white
3 specks master recipe
1 speck Naples yellow hue

4. 10 white
1 master recipe

MIDDLE VALUES

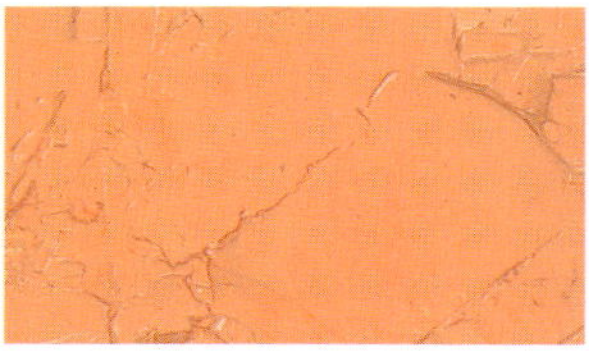

5. 8 white
1 master recipe

6. 6 white
1 master recipe

7. 5 white
2 master recipe
2 specks recipe #12

DARK/GRAYED VALUES

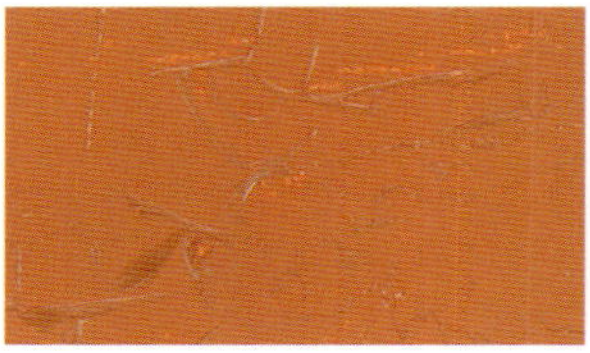

8. 3 white
1 master recipe
1 recipe #12

9. 2 white
1 master recipe
1 recipe #12
1 speck recipe #14

10. 1 white
1 master recipe
1 recipe #13
1 speck recipe #14

HIGHLIGHT VALUE

11. 1 white
2 specks Naples yellow hue

WARM SHADOW

12. 4 burnt sienna
1 white
1 master recipe

COOL SHADOW

13. 4 raw umber
1 white
1 master recipe

GRAYING COLOR

14. 2 viridian green
1 white
1 speck black

COLORS USED

- Burnt Umber
- Cadmium Red Light
- Cerulean Blue Hue
- Naples Yellow Hue
- Titanium White
- Venetian Red
- Yellow Ochre

Mix until the color matches the **Master Skin Tone Recipe** shown at right.

1. 5 cadmium red light
2 yellow ochre
3 white

Cadmium red light

Yellow ochre

White

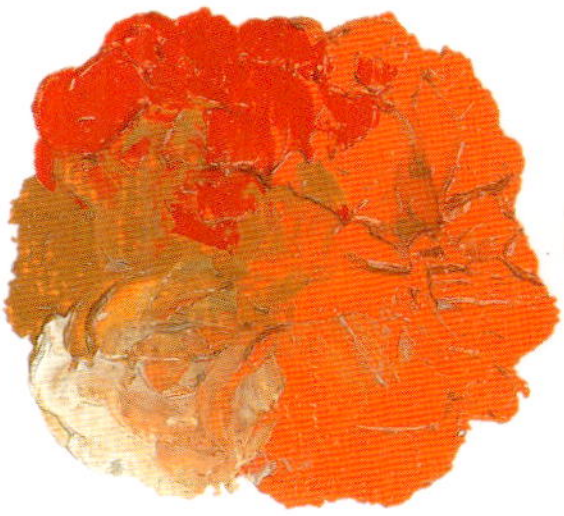

MASTER SKIN TONE RECIPE

LIGHT VALUES

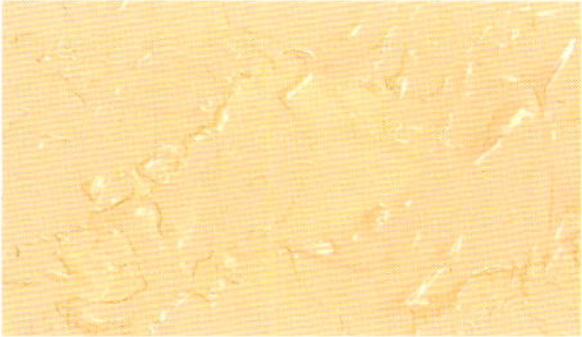

2. 9 white
1 Naples yellow hue

3. 2 recipe #2
1 speck Venetian red

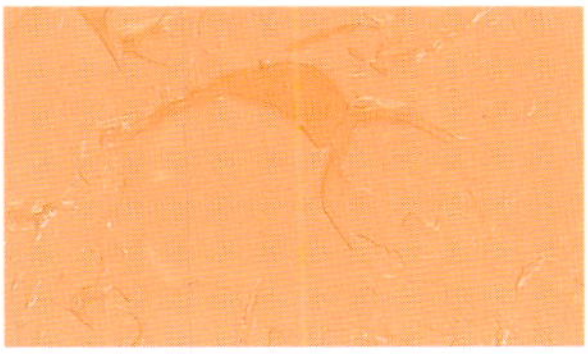

4. 13 recipe #2
1 master recipe

MIDDLE VALUES

5. 5 white
3 recipe #2
2 specks cadmium red light
1 speck master recipe

6. 6 white
1 recipe #2
1 master recipe
4 specks cadmium red light

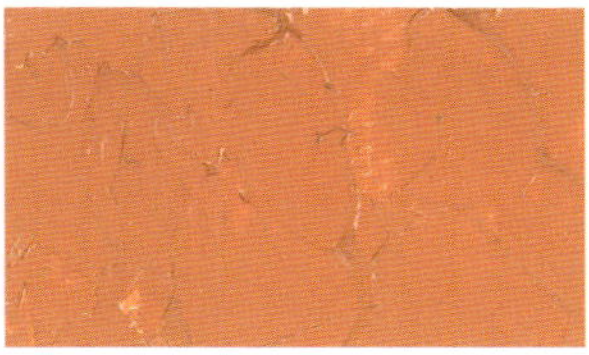

7. 4 recipe #5
3 specks Venetian red
1 speck master recipe

DARK/GRAYED VALUES

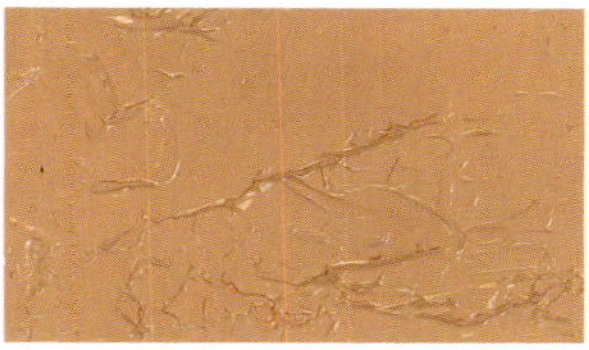

8. 7 white
2 master recipe
1 recipe #14
1 speck recipe #13

9. 5 recipe #8
1 master recipe
2 specks recipe #13

10. 5 recipe #9
1 recipe #12
1 recipe #14

HIGHLIGHT VALUE

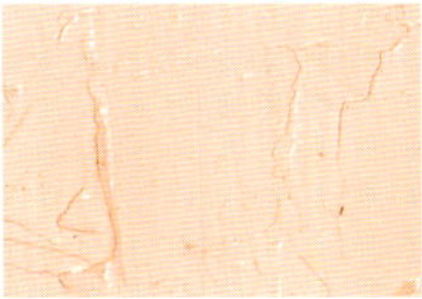

11. 2 white
1 speck cadmium red light

WARM SHADOW

12. 4 recipe #2
2 master recipe
1 Venetian red
1 burnt umber

COOL SHADOW

13. 2 master recipe
1 burnt umber

GRAYING COLOR

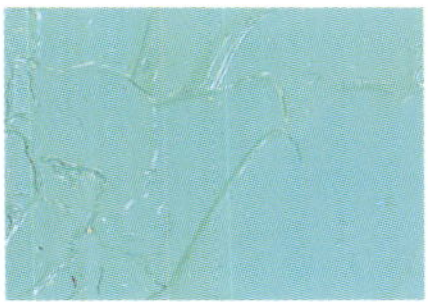

14. 4 white
1 cerulean blue hue

Skin Tone Recipes

COLORS USED

- Alizarin Crimson
- Cadmium Red Light
- Raw Sienna
- Titanium White
- Viridian Green

Mix until the color matches the **Master Skin Tone Recipe** shown at right.

1. 1 raw sienna
3 white

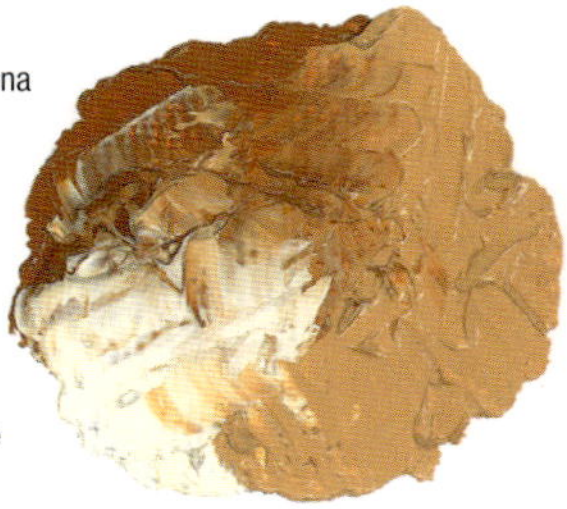

MASTER SKIN TONE RECIPE

LIGHT VALUES

2. 5 white
1 master recipe

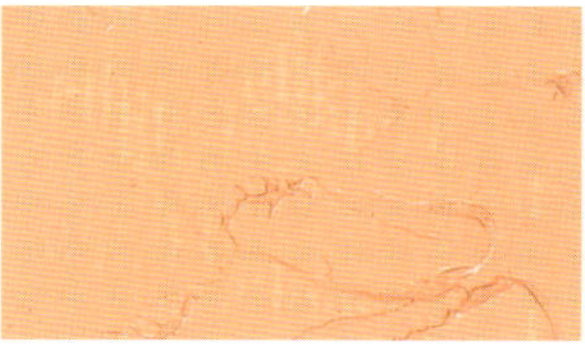

3. 5 recipe #2
3 specks cadmium red light

4. 1 recipe #3
1 speck alizarin crimson

MIDDLE VALUES

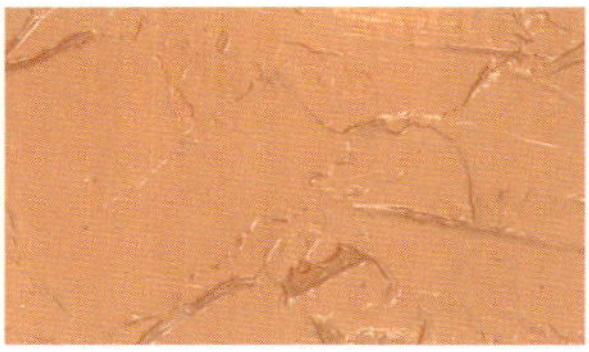

5. 1 white
1 master recipe
2 specks recipe #12

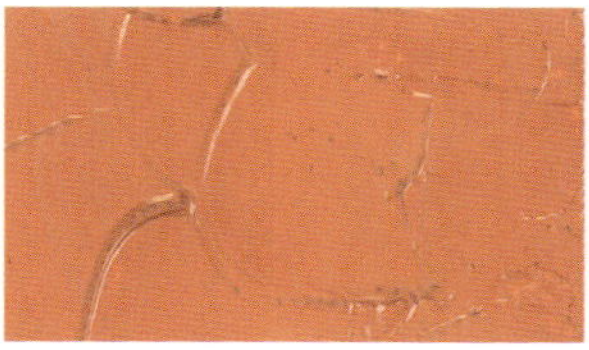

6. 3 white
5 master recipe
1 recipe #12

7. 6 recipe #6
1 recipe #13

DARK/GRAYED VALUES

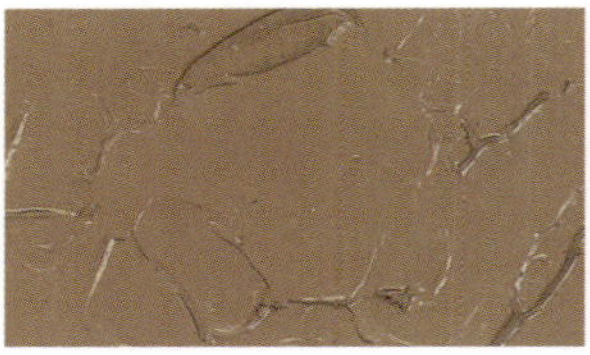

8. 3 recipe #7
1 recipe #14

9. 2 recipe #7
1 recipe #12
3 recipe #14
2 specks recipe #13

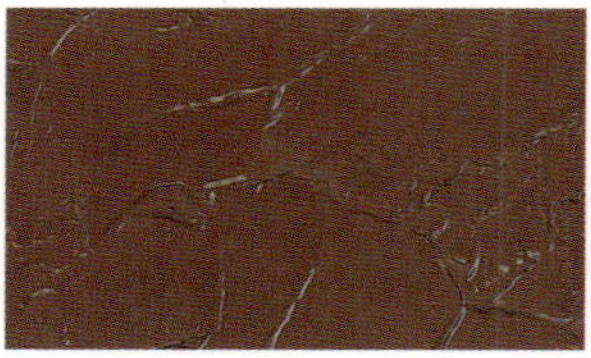

10. 5 recipe #9
3 recipe #13
1 speck raw sienna

HIGHLIGHT VALUE

11. 1 white
3 specks master recipe

WARM SHADOW

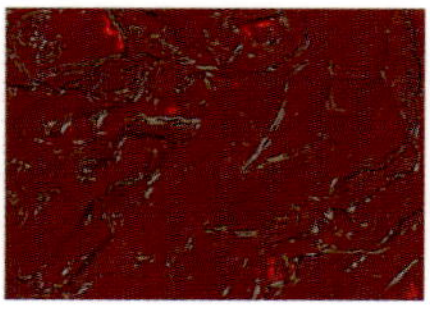

12. 1 raw sienna
1 alizarin crimson

COOL SHADOW

13. 1 raw sienna
1 alizarin crimson
1 viridian green

GRAYING COLOR

14. 3 white
1 viridian green

COLORS USED

- Burnt Umber
- Cobalt Blue
- Ivory Black
- Naples Yellow Hue
- Phthalo Red
- Titanium White
- Viridian Green

Mix until the color matches the **Master Skin Tone Recipe** shown at right.

1. 3 Naples yellow hue
1 phthalo red

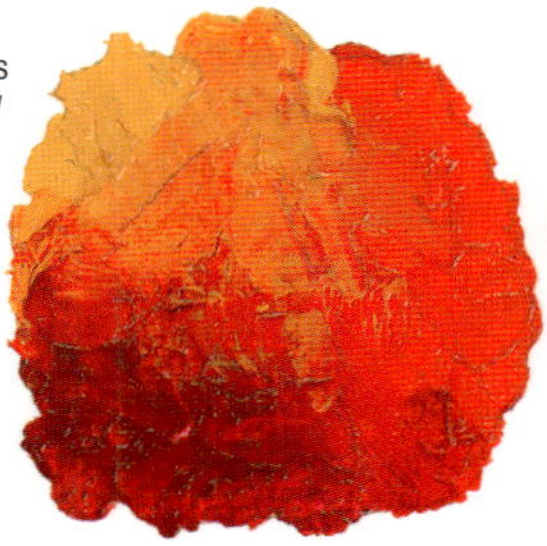

MASTER SKIN TONE RECIPE

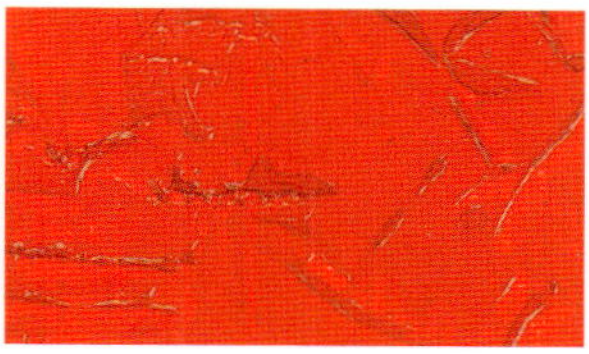

LIGHT VALUES

2. 2 white
1 speck master recipe
1 speck Naples yellow hue

3. 6 white
1 master recipe

4. 6 white
1 master recipe
1 Naples yellow hue

MIDDLE VALUES

5. 5 recipe #3
1 recipe #14

6. 7 white
1 master recipe
2 Naples yellow hue
1 recipe #12

7. 5 white
2 master recipe
1 Naples yellow hue
3 specks burnt umber

DARK/GRAYED VALUES

8. 1 master recipe
1 viridian green
1 recipe #11

9. 1 master recipe
1 recipe #13
1 recipe #14

10. 3 master recipe
1 white
2 recipe #13

HIGHLIGHT VALUE

11. 3 white
1 speck Naples yellow hue
1 tiny speck phthalo red

WARM SHADOW

12. 1 burnt umber
1 Naples yellow hue
1 phthalo red
2 white

COOL SHADOW

13. 3 master recipe
1 viridian green

GRAYING COLOR

14. 4 white
1 cobalt blue
1 speck black

SkinToneRecipes

COLORS USED

- Alizarin Crimson
- Burnt Sienna
- Burnt Umber
- Cerulean Blue Hue
- Naples Yellow Hue
- Raw Sienna
- Titanium White
- Viridian Green

Mix until the color matches the **Master Skin Tone Recipe** shown at right.

1. 1 raw sienna
1 alizarin crimson
1 white

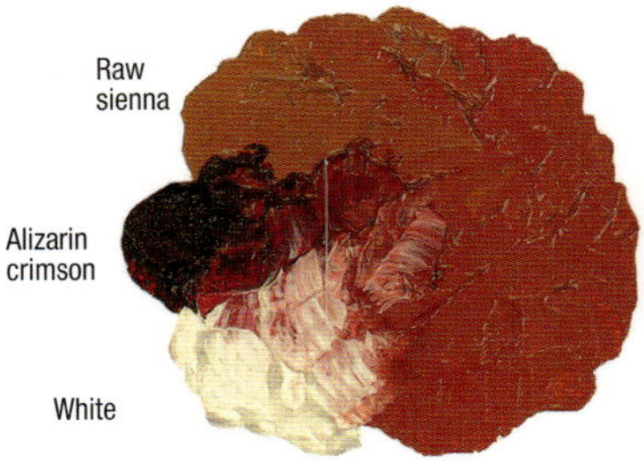

MASTER SKIN TONE RECIPE

LIGHT VALUES

2. 2 white
1 speck raw sienna

3. 3 white
1 speck Naples yellow hue
1 speck master recipe

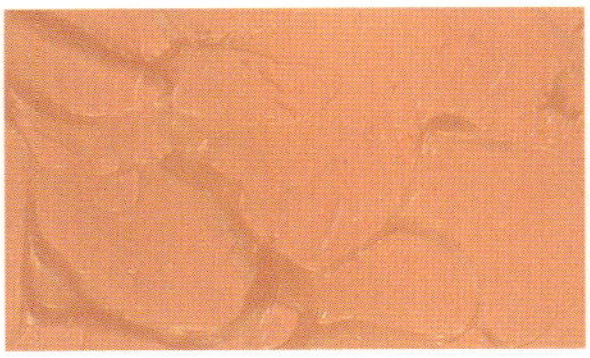

4. 9 white
1 master recipe
2 specks raw sienna

MIDDLE VALUES

5. 3 white
1 master recipe
2 specks raw sienna

6. 3 recipe #5
1 recipe #12

7. 3 recipe #5
1 burnt sienna
1 alizarin crimson
2 specks burnt umber

DARK/GRAYED VALUES

8. 6 master recipe
3 white
2 recipe #13

9. 3 recipe #8
1 recipe #14

10. 2 master recipe
3 burnt umber
1 burnt sienna
1 alizarin crimson

HIGHLIGHT VALUE

11. 1 white
1 speck Naples yellow hue

WARM SHADOW

12. 3 master recipe
1 burnt umber

COOL SHADOW

13. 3 master recipe
2 viridian green

GRAYING COLOR

14. 1 cerulean blue hue
1 viridian green
1 white

SkinToneRecipes

COLORS USED

- Burnt Sienna
- Cadmium Orange
- Cadmium Red Light
- Cadmium Vermilion
- Cadmium Yellow Medium
- Cerulean Blue Hue
- Raw Sienna
- Titanium White
- Viridian Green

Mix until the color matches the **Master Skin Tone Recipe** shown at right.

1. 5 raw sienna
2 cadmium red light

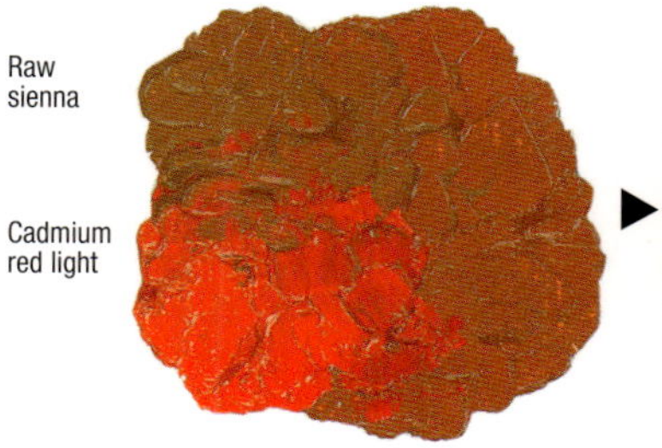

MASTER SKIN TONE RECIPE

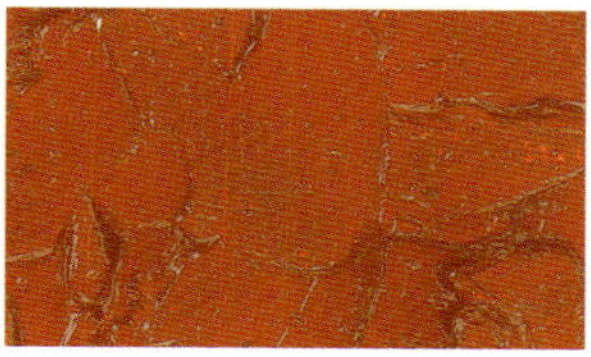

LIGHT VALUES

2. 2 white
1 speck master recipe
2 specks recipe #11

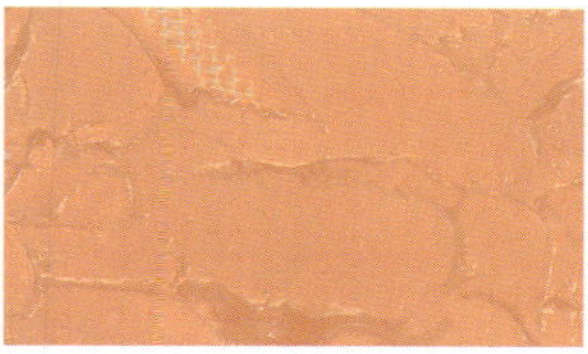

3. 10 white
1 master recipe

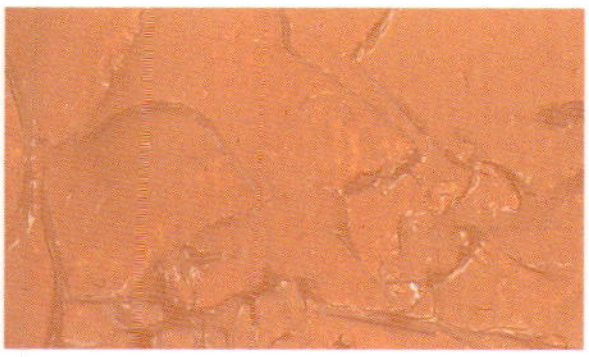

4. 6 white
1 master recipe

MIDDLE VALUES

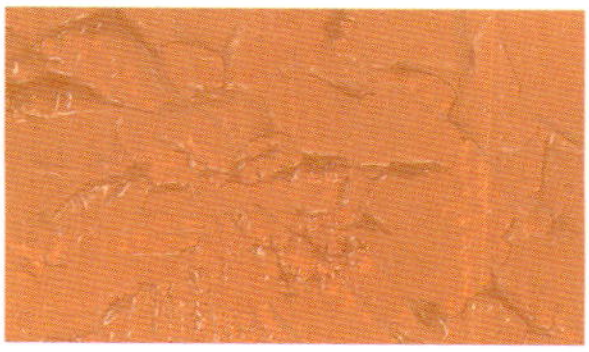

5. 3 white
1 master recipe
1 speck cadmium orange

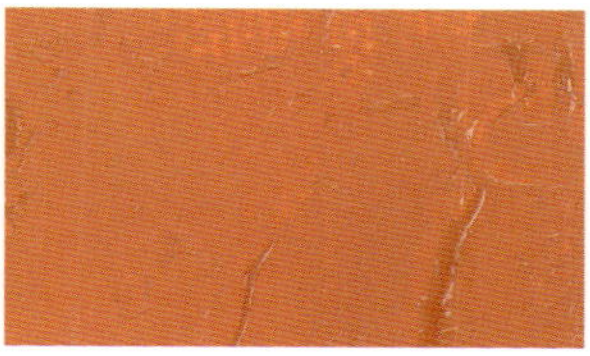

6. 2 white
1 master recipe
2 specks cadmium vermilion

7. 2 white
1 master recipe
1 cadmium vermilion

DARK/GRAYED VALUES

8. 1 white
1 master recipe
1 recipe #12

9. 1 master recipe
1 recipe #13

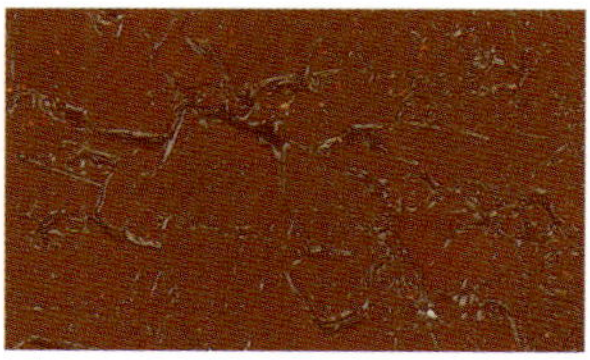

10. 1 master recipe
2 recipe #14
1 speck cadmium vermilion

HIGHLIGHT VALUE

11. 1 white
1 speck cadmium yellow medium

WARM SHADOW

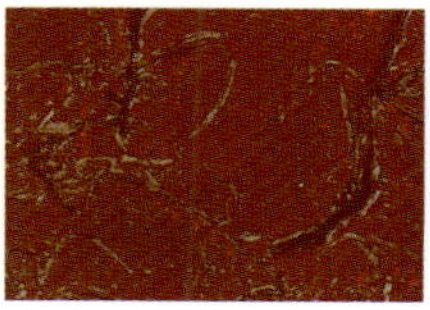

12. 1 master recipe
1 burnt sienna

COOL SHADOW

13. 1 white
1 cerulean blue hue
1 cadmium vermilion

GRAYING COLOR

14. 2 master recipe
1 viridian green

SkinToneRecipes

COLORS USED

- Alizarin Crimson
- Burnt Sienna
- Burnt Umber
- Cadmium Orange
- Cadmium Yellow Medium
- Naples Yellow Hue
- Phthalo Red
- Raw Sienna
- Titanium White
- Ultramarine Blue

Mix until the color matches the **Master Skin Tone Recipe** shown at right.

1. 6 Naples yellow hue
1 cadmium yellow medium
1 raw sienna
1 speck phthalo red

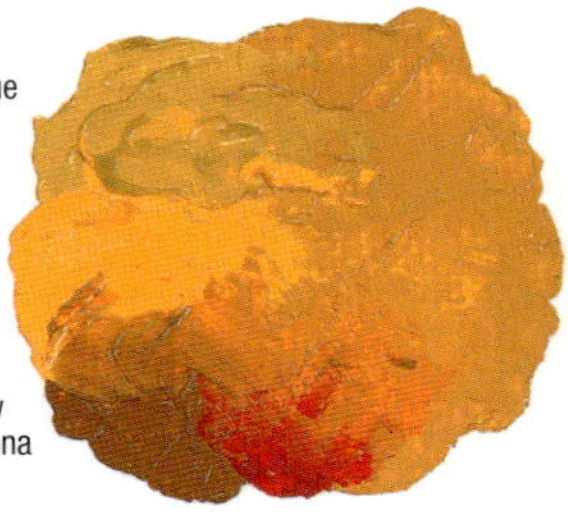

MASTER SKIN TONE RECIPE

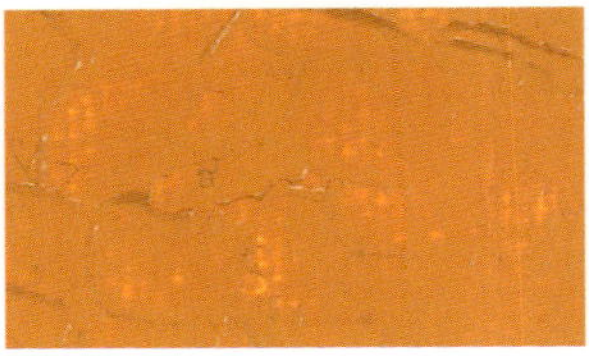

LIGHT VALUES

2. 2 white
1 speck master recipe

3. 1 recipe #2
1 recipe #4

4. 3 white
1 master recipe

MIDDLE VALUES

5. 8 white
2 master recipe
1 cadmium orange

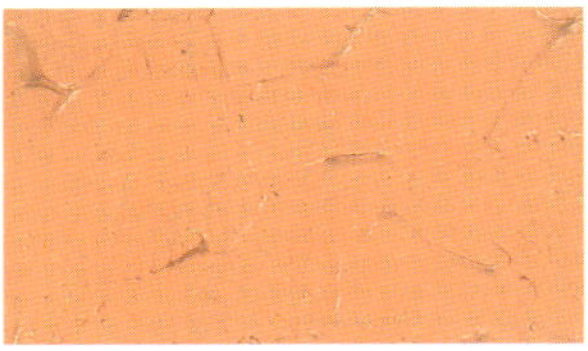

6. 1 recipe #5
1 speck phthalo red

7. 2 recipe #6
2 specks recipe #14

DARK/GRAYED VALUES

8. 2 master recipe
1 recipe #14
1 speck phthalo red

9. 3 master recipe
1 recipe #14
1 recipe #12

10. 4 master recipe
1 recipe #13
1 recipe #11

HIGHLIGHT VALUE

11. 2 white
1 speck cadmium yellow medium

WARM SHADOW

12. 1 white
2 burnt sienna

COOL SHADOW

13. 1 white
1 burnt umber
1 alizarin crimson

GRAYING COLOR

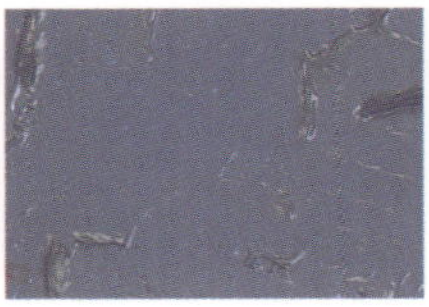

14. 3 white
1 ultramarine blue
3 specks alizarin crimson

COLORS USED

- Alizarin Crimson
- Burnt Sienna
- Burnt Umber
- Cadmium Orange
- Cadmium Vermilion
- Cadmium Yellow Medium
- Ivory Black
- Naples Yellow Hue
- Raw Sienna
- Titanium White
- Ultramarine Blue

Mix until the color matches the **Master Skin Tone Recipe** shown at right.

1. 8 Naples yellow hue
1 cadmium yellow medium
3 raw sienna
2 specks cadmium vermilion

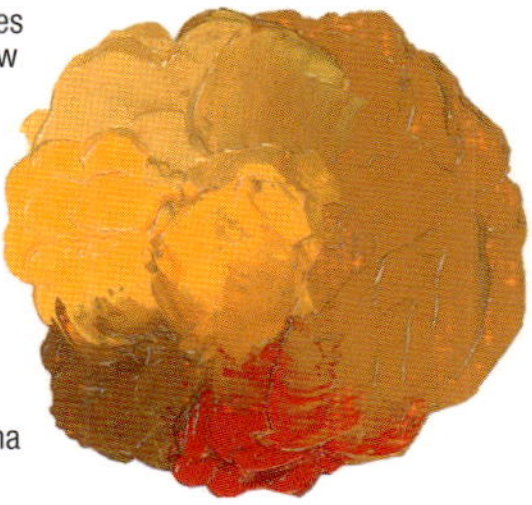

MASTER SKIN TONE RECIPE

LIGHT VALUES

2. 2 white
1 speck master recipe

3. 1 recipe #2
1 recipe #4

4. 2 white
1 master recipe

MIDDLE VALUES

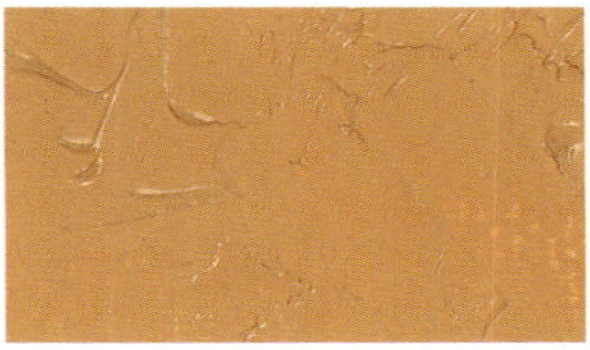

5. 2 white
1 master recipe
1 burnt sienna
1 recipe #11

6. 5 recipe #5
1 cadmium orange
1 recipe #12

7. 2 recipe #5
1 recipe #13

DARK/GRAYED VALUES

8. 3 master recipe
2 specks cadmium vermilion
1 speck alizarin crimson

9. 2 master recipe
1 recipe #13

10. 6 master recipe
1 alizarin crimson
3 specks ultramarine blue

HIGHLIGHT VALUE

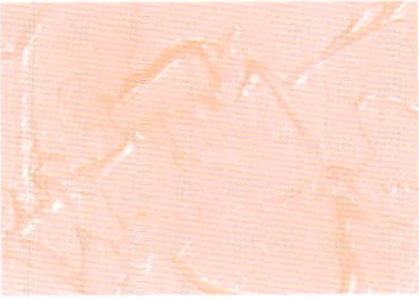

11. 1 white
1 speck cadmium vermilion

WARM SHADOW

12. 2 white
2 burnt sienna
1 black

COOL SHADOW

13. 2 white
2 burnt umber
1 alizarin crimson

GRAYING COLOR

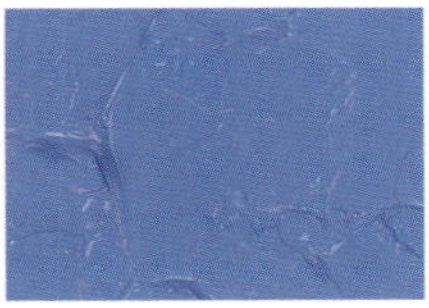

14. 2 white
1 ultramarine blue

SkinToneRecipes

COLORS USED

- Alizarin Crimson
- Burnt Sienna
- Burnt Umber
- Cadmium Orange
- Cadmium Vermilion
- Naples Yellow Hue
- Raw Sienna
- Titanium White
- Ultramarine Blue

Mix until the color matches the **Master Skin Tone Recipe** shown at right.

1. 1 raw sienna
1 cadmium orange
1 white

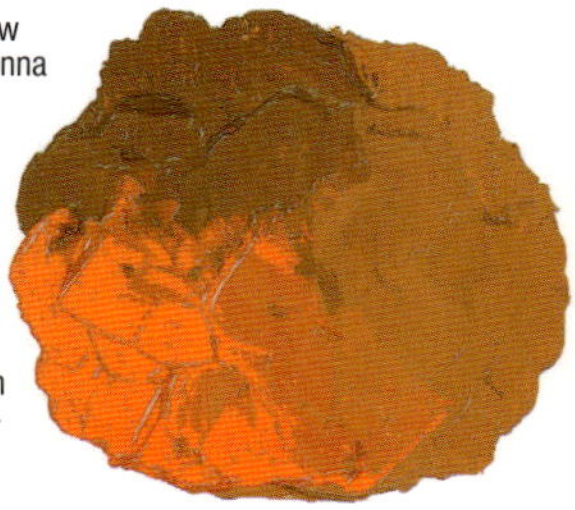

MASTER SKIN TONE RECIPE

LIGHT VALUES

2. 2 recipe #11
1 speck master recipe

3. 2 white
1 master recipe

4. 1 recipe #3
1 speck burnt sienna
1 speck cadmium vermilion

MIDDLE VALUES

5. 2 master recipe
1 white
2 specks cadmium vermilion

6. 2 recipe #5
1 recipe #12

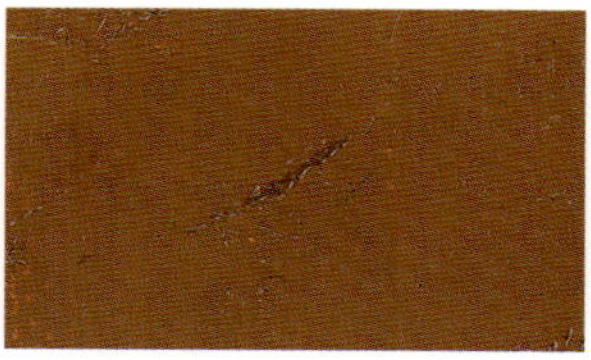

7. 2 recipe #5
1 recipe #13

DARK/GRAYED VALUES

8. 2 master recipe
1 burnt umber
1 cadmium orange

9. 1 master recipe
1 recipe #12

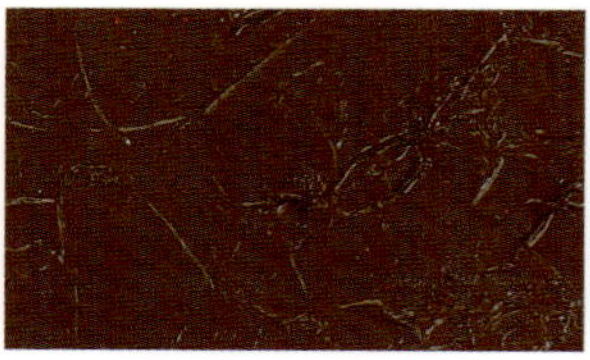

10. 1 master recipe
1 recipe #12
1 recipe #13
1 speck #14

HIGHLIGHT VALUE

11. 3 white
1 speck cadmium orange

WARM SHADOW

12. 2 burnt sienna
1 alizarin crimson
1 Naples yellow hue

COOL SHADOW

13. 2 burnt umber
1 alizarin crimson
1 Naples yellow hue

GRAYING COLOR

14. 1 white
1 ultramarine blue
1 alizarin crimson

COLORS USED

- Alizarin Crimson
- Burnt Umber
- Burnt Sienna
- Cadmium Red Light
- Cadmium Vermilion
- Chrome Oxide Green
- Cobalt Blue
- Titanium White
- Yellow Ochre

Mix until the color matches the **Master Skin Tone Recipe** shown at right.

1. 4 yellow ochre
2 burnt sienna
1 chrome oxide green
3 cadmium red light

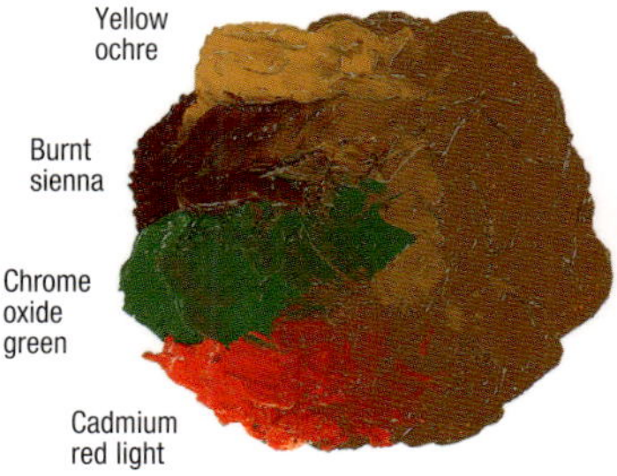

MASTER SKIN TONE RECIPE

LIGHT VALUES

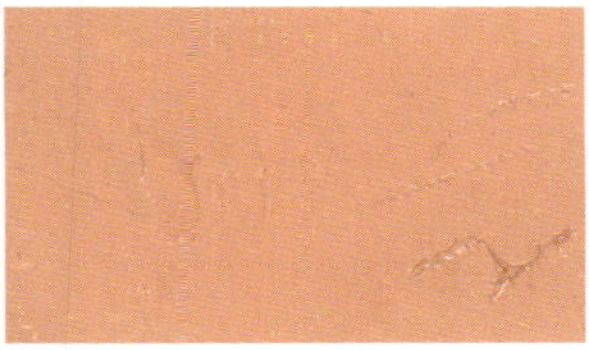

2. 1 recipe #11
1 speck master recipe

3. 3 white
1 master recipe

4. 3 white
1 master recipe
2 specks cadmium vermilion

MIDDLE VALUES

5. 4 white
1 master recipe

6. 1 recipe #5
1 recipe #7

7. 3 recipe #5
1 master recipe

DARK/GRAYED VALUES

8. 2 recipe #4
1 recipe #12

9. 2 recipe #11
1 master recipe
1 recipe #14

10. 2 recipe #9
1 recipe #13

HIGHLIGHT VALUE

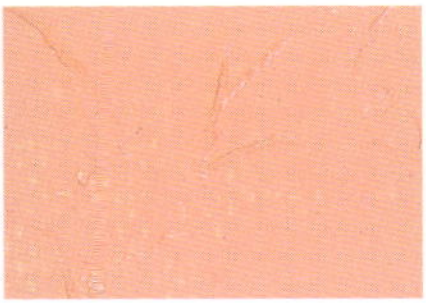

11. 1 white
1 speck cadmium vermilion

WARM SHADOW

12. 2 master recipe
1 burnt sienna
1 speck alizarin crimson

COOL SHADOW

13. 2 master recipe
1 burnt umber

GRAYING COLOR

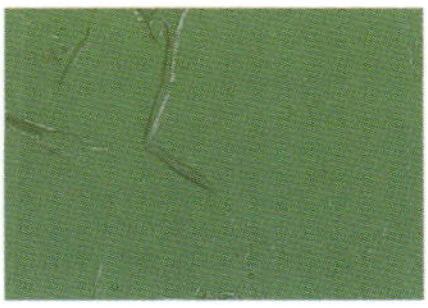

14. 2 white
1 chrome oxide green
2 specks cobalt blue

SkinToneRecipes

COLORS USED

- Alizarin Crimson
- Burnt Umber
- Burnt Sienna
- Cadmium Orange
- Cadmium Vermilion
- Cadmium Yellow Medium
- Ivory Black
- Titanium White
- Ultramarine Blue
- Yellow Ochre

Mix until the color matches the **Master Skin Tone Recipe** shown at right.

1. 2 white
1 yellow ochre
2 burnt sienna
1 black

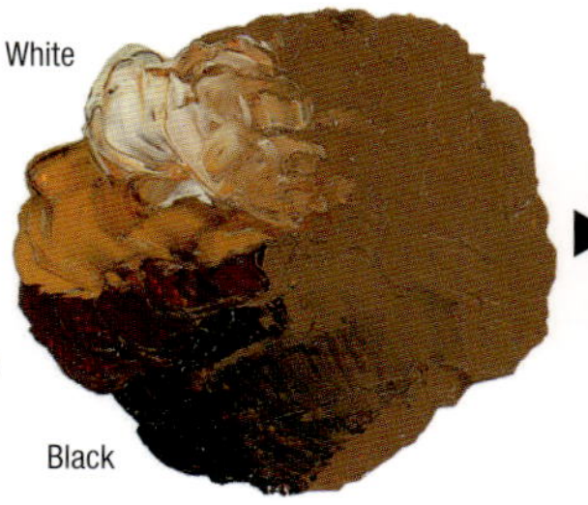

MASTER SKIN TONE RECIPE

LIGHT VALUES

2. 2 white
1 recipe #11
1 speck master recipe

3. 1 master recipe
1 white
1 recipe #11

4. 2 recipe #3
1 master recipe

MIDDLE VALUES

5. 1 white
1 master recipe
2 specks recipe #12

6. 2 white
3 master recipe
3 specks cadmium vermilion

7. 2 master recipe
1 burnt sienna

DARK/GRAYED VALUES

8. 6 recipe #14
2 master recipe
1 cadmium vermilion

9. 4 master recipe
2 recipe #14
1 alizarin crimson

10. 2 master recipe
1 recipe #13

HIGHLIGHT VALUE

11. 3 white
1 speck cadmium orange
1 speck cadmium yellow medium

WARM SHADOW

12. 2 burnt umber
1 cadmium vermilion

COOL SHADOW

13. 2 white
1 black
1 burnt umber
1 speck alizarin crimson

GRAYING COLOR

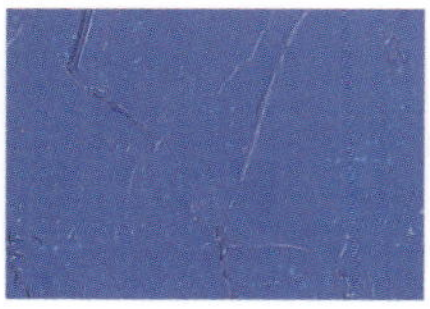

14. 2 white
1 ultramarine blue

COLORS USED

- Alizarin Crimson
- Burnt Sienna
- Burnt Umber
- Cadmium Orange
- Cadmium Red Light
- Cadmium Yellow Medium
- Naples Yellow Hue
- Raw Sienna
- Titanium White
- Ultramarine Blue

Mix until the color matches the **Master Skin Tone Recipe** shown at right.

1. 4 Naples yellow hue
1 burnt sienna
3 specks cadmium orange

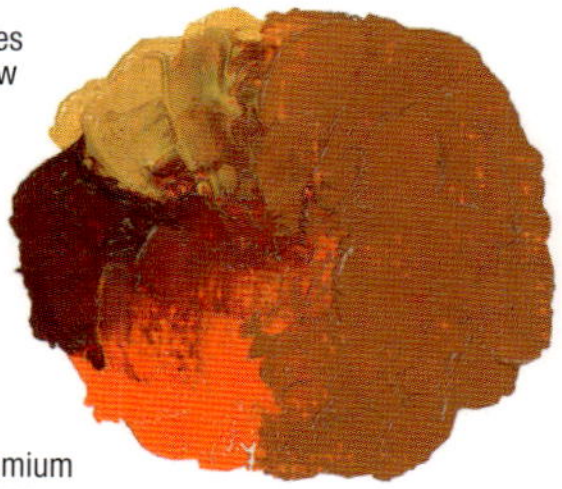

MASTER SKIN TONE RECIPE

LIGHT VALUES

2. 1 white
1 recipe #11
1 speck master recipe

3. 2 white
2 recipe #11
1 master recipe

4. 3 recipe #11
1 master recipe

MIDDLE VALUES

5. 3 recipe #14
1 master recipe
1 speck cadmium orange

6. 1 recipe #14
1 master recipe
1 speck recipe #12

7. 3 master recipe
1 recipe #12

DARK/GRAYED VALUES

8. 2 master recipe
1 recipe #14

9. 2 master recipe
1 recipe #12
1 speck cadmium red light

10. 1 master recipe
1 recipe #13

HIGHLIGHT VALUE

11. 3 white
1 Naples yellow hue
1 speck cadmium yellow medium

WARM SHADOW

12. 2 burnt umber
1 alizarin crimson
1 raw sienna

COOL SHADOW

13. 1 burnt umber
1 speck cadmium orange

GRAYING COLOR

14. 1 white
1 ultramarine blue
1 alizarin crimson

SkinToneRecipes

COLORS USED

- Burnt Sienna
- Burnt Umber
- Cadmium Red Light
- Cobalt Blue
- Ivory Black
- Naples Yellow Hue
- Titanium White
- Venetian Red
- Viridian Green

Mix until the color matches the **Master Skin Tone Recipe** shown at right.

1. 3 Venetian red
1 burnt sienna

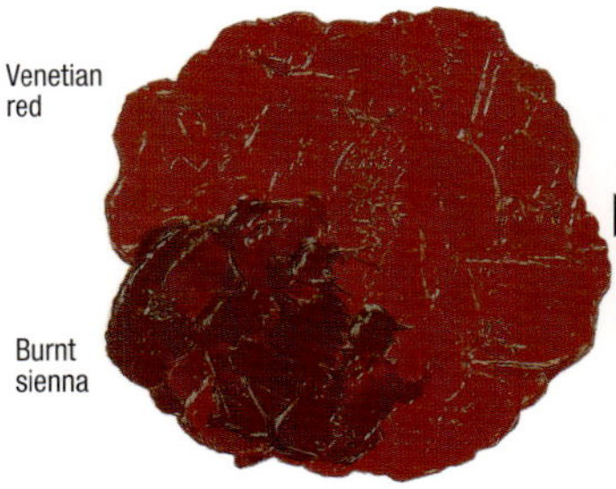

MASTER SKIN TONE RECIPE

LIGHT VALUES

2. 1 Naples yellow hue
1 speck master recipe
1 speck cadmium red light

3. 1 recipe #11
1 speck master recipe

4. 1 recipe #11
2 specks master recipe

MIDDLE VALUES

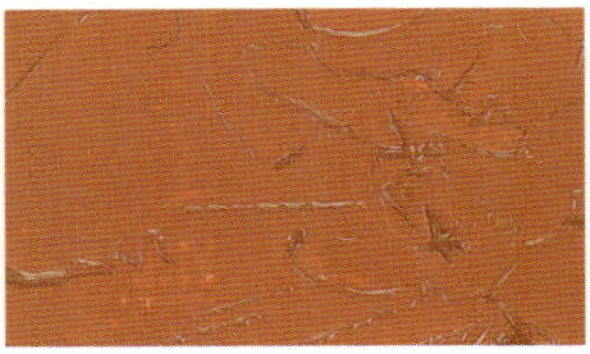

5. 1 recipe #11
4 specks master recipe

6. 4 recipe #11
1 master recipe
3 Naples yellow hue

7. 2 recipe #11
1 master recipe

DARK/GRAYED VALUES

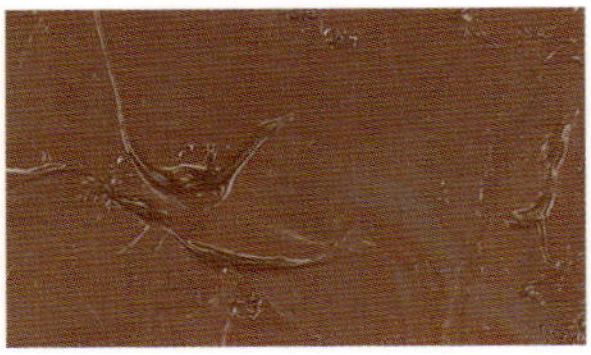

8. 5 recipe #14
1 master recipe

9. 1 white
1 master recipe
1 recipe #12

10. 3 recipe #13
1 master recipe
2 recipe #14

HIGHLIGHT VALUE

11. 6 white
5 Naples yellow hue
1 cadmium red light

WARM SHADOW

12. 1 master recipe
2 burnt umber

COOL SHADOW

13. 2 black
3 viridian green
1 master recipe

GRAYING COLOR

14. 2 white
1 cobalt blue

Skin Tone Recipes

COLORS USED

- Alizarin Crimson
- Burnt Sienna
- Burnt Umber
- Cadmium Orange
- Cadmium Red Light
- Cadmium Yellow Medium
- Chrome Oxide Green
- Raw Sienna
- Titanium White
- Viridian Green

Mix until the color matches the **Master Skin Tone Recipe** shown at right.

1. 3 burnt sienna
2 raw sienna
1 speck cadmium red light

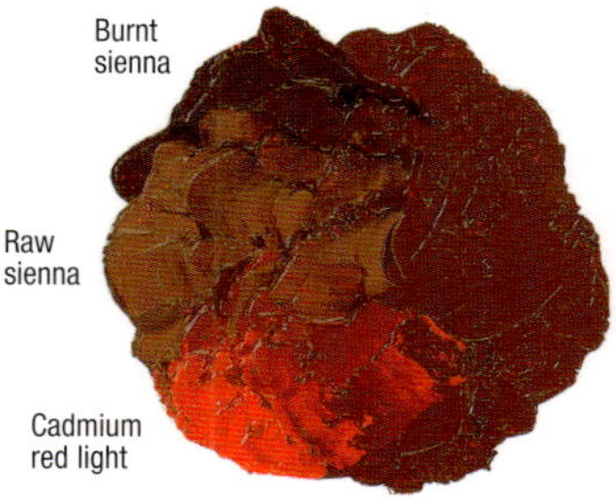

MASTER SKIN TONE RECIPE

LIGHT VALUES

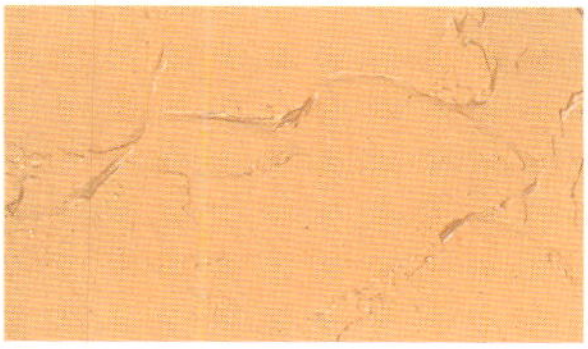

2. 2 white
1 recipe #11
1 speck master recipe

3. 1 recipe #11
2 specks master recipe

4. 2 recipe #11
1 master recipe

MIDDLE VALUES

5. 1 white
1 master recipe

6. 3 recipe #5
1 recipe #12

7. 1 recipe #6
1 recipe #12
1 speck cadmium orange

DARK/GRAYED VALUES

8. 4 master recipe
1 recipe #14

9. 1 master recipe
1 recipe #12

10. 1 master recipe
1 recipe #13

HIGHLIGHT VALUE

11. 5 white
1 cadmium yellow medium
1 speck cadmium red light

WARM SHADOW

12. 2 burnt umber
1 alizarin crimson

COOL SHADOW

13. 2 burnt sienna
3 viridian green

GRAYING COLOR

14. 1 white
1 chrome oxide green

SkinToneRecipes

COLORS USED

- Alizarin Crimson
- Burnt Sienna
- Burnt Umber
- Cadmium Orange
- Cadmium Vermilion
- Ivory Black
- Titanium White
- Ultramarine Blue
- Yellow Ochre

Mix until the color matches the **Master Skin Tone Recipe** shown at right.

1. 2 burnt sienna
2 cadmium orange
1 yellow ochre
1 burnt umber

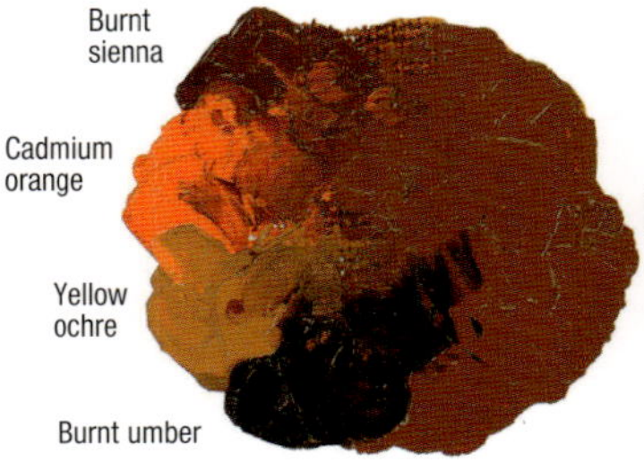

MASTER SKIN TONE RECIPE

LIGHT VALUES

2. 1 recipe #11
1 speck master recipe

3. 1 recipe #11
1 master recipe

4. 1 recipe #11
1 master recipe
2 specks alizarin crimson

MIDDLE VALUES

5. 1 recipe #11
1 master recipe
3 specks alizarin crimson
2 specks recipe #12

6. 1 recipe #5
1 recipe #7

7. 1 master recipe
1 burnt sienna

DARK/GRAYED VALUES

8. 1 master recipe
1 recipe #14

9. 1 master recipe
1 recipe #12
1 speck recipe #14

10. 2 master recipe
1 recipe #13

HIGHLIGHT VALUE

11. 1 white
1 yellow ochre
1 cadmium orange

WARM SHADOW

12. 2 burnt sienna
1 burnt umber

COOL SHADOW

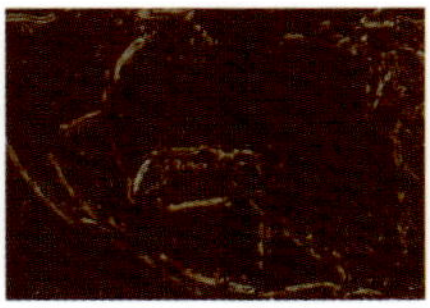

13. 2 black
1 cadmium vermilion

GRAYING COLOR

14. 2 white
1 ultramarine blue
1 alizarin crimson

Skin Tone Recipes

COLORS USED

- Alizarin Crimson
- Burnt Sienna
- Burnt Umber
- Cadmium Orange
- Cadmium Red Light
- Cadmium Vermilion
- Ivory Black
- Naples Yellow Hue
- Titanium White
- Ultramarine Blue
- Yellow Ochre

Mix until the color matches the **Master Skin Tone Recipe** shown at right.

1. 4 Naples yellow hue
2 burnt sienna
1 cadmium orange
1 white

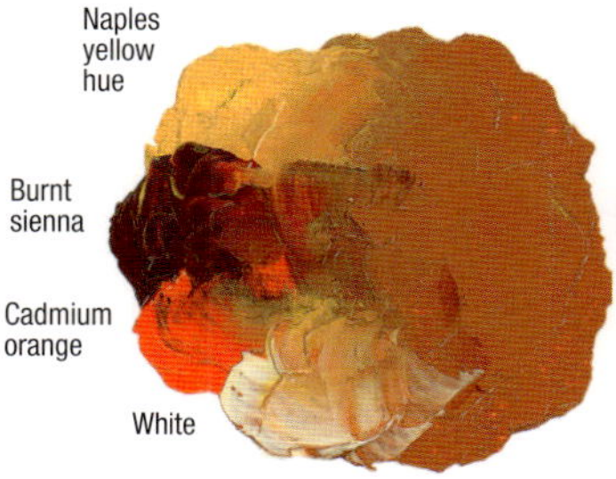

MASTER SKIN TONE RECIPE

LIGHT VALUES

2. 1 recipe #11
1 speck master recipe

3. 1 recipe #11
1 master recipe

4. 2 master recipe
3 recipe #11
2 specks alizarin crimson
2 specks burnt umber

MIDDLE VALUES

5. 3 master recipe
1 burnt umber

6. 3 master recipe
1 cadmium vermilion
1 recipe #14

7. 5 recipe #14
1 master recipe
1 recipe #12

DARK/GRAYED VALUES

8. 1 master recipe
1 recipe #14

9. 2 master recipe
1 recipe #12
1 recipe #14

10. 2 master recipe
1 recipe #13

HIGHLIGHT VALUE

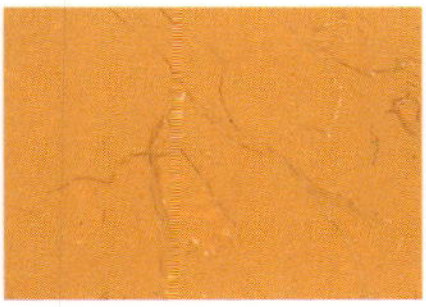

11. 2 white
1 Naples yellow hue
1 yellow ochre
1 speck cadmium red light

WARM SHADOW

12. 3 burnt sienna
1 black
2 specks cadmium vermilion

COOL SHADOW

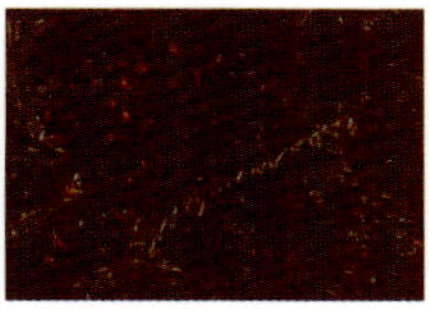

13. 3 burnt umber
2 alizarin crimson

GRAYING COLOR

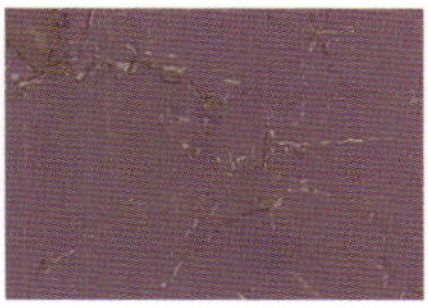

14. 4 white
1 alizarin crimson
1 ultramarine blue

SkinToneRecipes

COLORS USED

- Alizarin Crimson
- Burnt Sienna
- Burnt Umber
- Cadmium Orange
- Cobalt Blue
- Ivory Black
- Raw Umber
- Titanium White
- Venetian Red
- Viridian Green

Mix until the color matches the **Master Skin Tone Recipe** shown at right.

1. 2 raw umber
1 burnt sienna
3 white

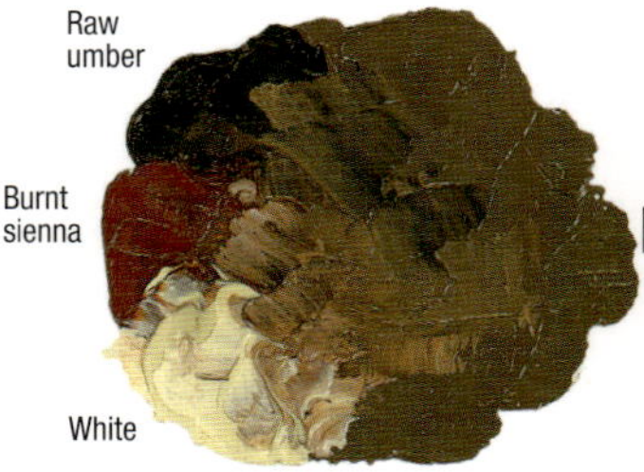

MASTER SKIN TONE RECIPE

LIGHT VALUES

2. 3 white
1 recipe #11
1 master recipe

3. 2 recipe #11
2 white
1 master recipe

4. 3 recipe #11
1 master recipe

MIDDLE VALUES

5. 1 master recipe
2 white
1 speck alizarin crimson

6. 1 recipe #5
2 specks black

7. 1 recipe #6
2 specks black
2 specks burnt umber

DARK/GRAYED VALUES

8. 2 master recipe
1 recipe #12

9. 2 master recipe
1 recipe #13

10. 2 master recipe
1 viridian green

HIGHLIGHT VALUE

11. 3 white
1 alizarin crimson
1 cadmium orange

WARM SHADOW

12. 2 black
1 Venetian red

COOL SHADOW

13. 1 black
1 cobalt blue

GRAYING COLOR

14. Viridian green (pure)

COLORS USED

- Alizarin Crimson
- Burnt Sienna
- Burnt Umber
- Cadmium Orange
- Cadmium Red Light
- Cobalt Blue
- Raw Umber
- Titanium White

Mix until the color matches the **Master Skin Tone Recipe** shown at right.

1. 2 raw umber
1 burnt sienna
6 white

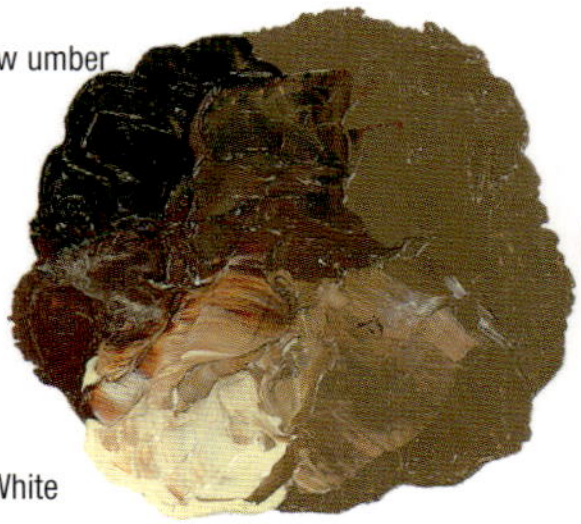

MASTER SKIN TONE RECIPE

LIGHT VALUES

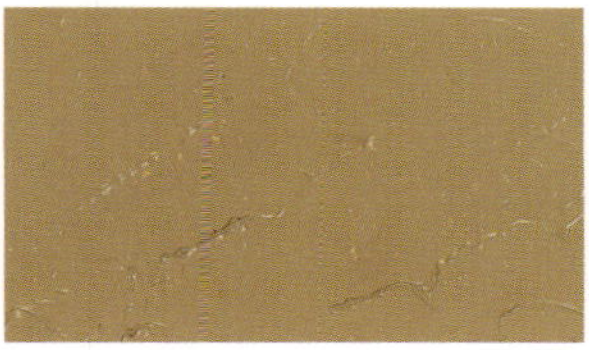

2. 5 white
1 master recipe
1 recipe #1

3. 2 master recipe
2 recipe #11
3 white

4. 1 recipe #3
2 specks alizarin crimson

MIDDLE VALUES

5. 4 white
1 master recipe
1 burnt sienna
1 recipe #11

6. 2 recipe #5
1 white
1 burnt sienna

7. 1 white
1 recipe #6
2 specks alizarin crimson

DARK/GRAYED VALUES

8. 1 master recipe
1 recipe #14

9. 2 white
2 master recipe
1 recipe #12

10. 3 white
2 master recipe
1 recipe #13

HIGHLIGHT VALUE

11. 3 white
1 cadmium orange
1 speck cadmium red light

WARM SHADOW

12. 1 burnt sienna
1 speck cobalt blue

COOL SHADOW

13. Burnt umber (pure)

GRAYING COLOR

14. 12 white
4 cobalt blue
1 cadmium red light

ColorTones EYES

BASIC COLOR RECIPES FOR THE EYES

The basic color recipes in this book offer good starting mixes that can be lightened, darkened, or grayed according to your model.

THE UPPER LID CASTS A SHADOW ON THE EYEBALL.

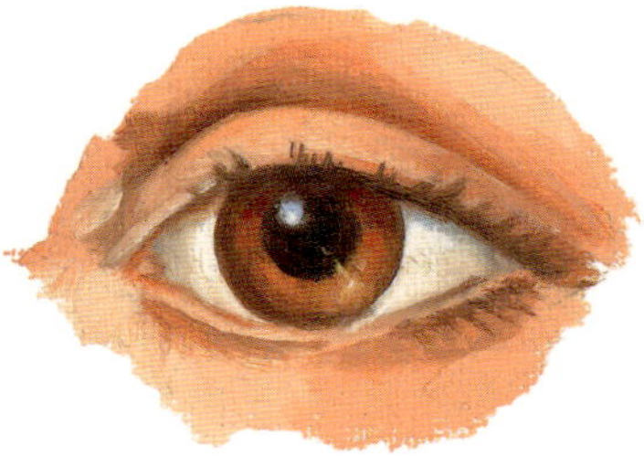

The white of the eye is not pure white. Mix a bit of skin tone and a tiny bit of ultramarine blue into white. Keep the mix warm and light. Then highlight a small area on each side of the iris with a spot of pure white. The surface reflection on the eye should be soft. Paint a light blue circle first (white + 1 speck of ultramarine blue), and then place the white highlight spot in it. Titanium white and flake white are both warm whites and work well for skin tones and eyes in portrait painting.

BROWN

Eyes in this book are lit from the upper left. Light is caught in the lower right of the iris, creating a liquid appearance and a reflection on the surface in the upper left pupil.

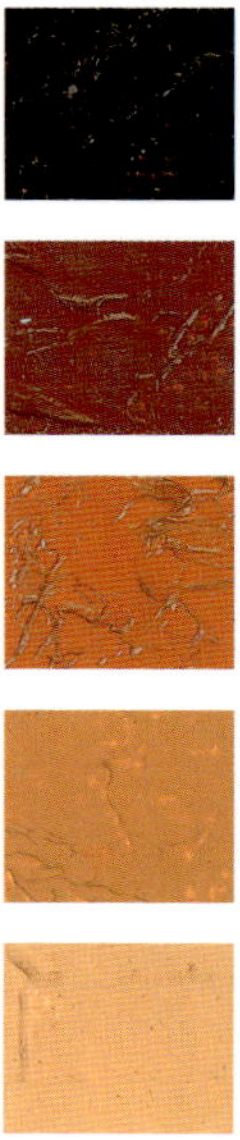

1. Pupil
1 burnt umber +
1 speck ultramarine blue

2. Iris Main
2 burnt sienna +
1 raw sienna

3. Iris Medium
3 recipe #2 +
5 yellow ochre +
2 cadmium orange

4. Iris Light
3 yellow ochre +
2 white +
1 recipe #3

5. Iris Highlight
2 white + 1 speck yellow ochre +
1 speck recipe #4

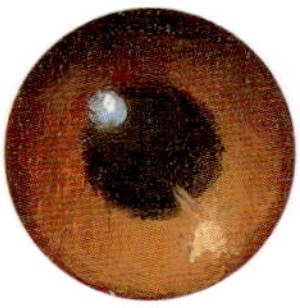

MAIN COLOR BLENDS

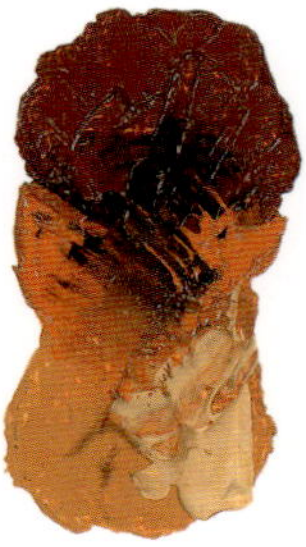

LIGHT BROWN

There is a wide range of light brown eyes. Warm these colors with a tiny speck of cadmium red light, or cool them with a speck of ultramarine blue.

1. Pupil
1 burnt sienna +
1 speck burnt umber

2. Iris Main
2 raw sienna +
1 speck cadmium red light

3. Iris Medium
4 Naples yellow hue +
1 raw sienna

4. Iris Light
1 Naples yellow hue + 1 speck cadmium orange

5. Iris Highlight
2 white +
1 recipe #4

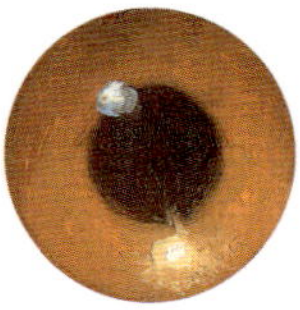

MAIN COLOR BLENDS

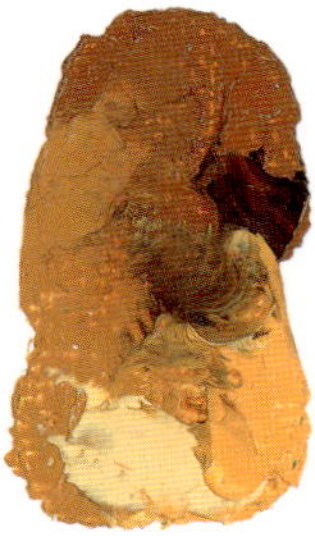

DARK BROWN

Keep all dark brown mixes warm in color tone. As with all the eyes, the iris is darker at the top because of the shadow cast by the upper eyelid and lashes.

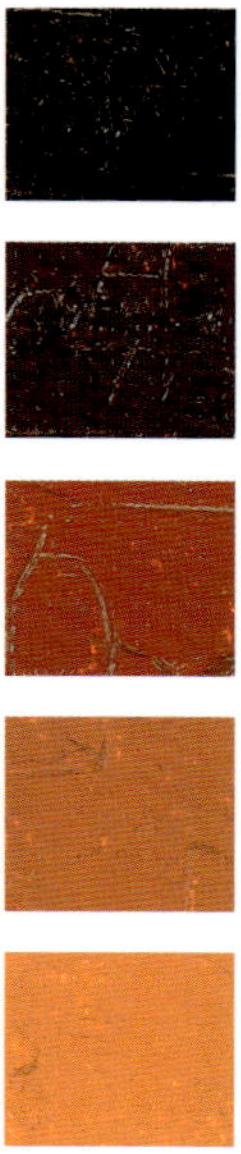

1. Pupil
2 burnt umber +
1 black

2. Iris Main
1 burnt umber +
1 burnt sienna

3. Iris Medium
1 burnt umber +
1 cadmium orange

4. Iris Light
1 recipe #3 +
1 white

5. Iris Highlight
1 yellow ochre +
1 cadmium orange
+ 1 white

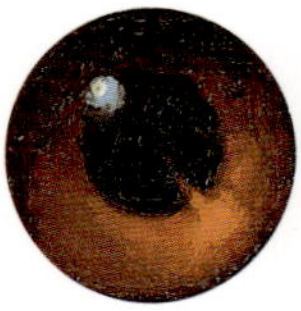

MAIN COLOR BLENDS

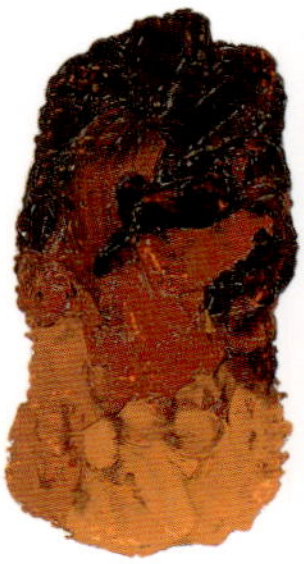

BLUE

Blue eyes can range from a light crystal color to a deep sapphire. The basic recipes here can be lightened with white; darkened with deeper blues, such as cobalt or ultramarine blue; or grayed with burnt umber, raw sienna, or a speck of cadmium orange.

1. Pupil
1 black +
1 ultramarine blue
+ 1 recipe #2

2. Iris Main
2 white + 1 ultramarine blue + 1 speck cadmium red light

3. Iris Medium
3 white +
1 cerulean blue hue
+ 1 recipe #2

4. Iris Light
2 white +
1 recipe #3

5. Iris Highlight
2 white +
1 speck Naples yellow hue

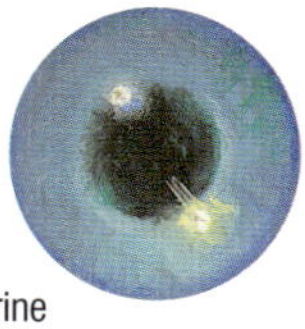

MAIN COLOR BLENDS

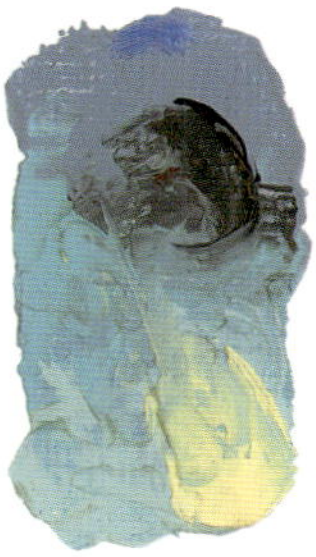

GREEN

There are many variations of green eyes—some even appear to have small flecks of brown or yellow. Use raw sienna and yellow ochre warmed with a speck of cadmium orange to create this effect.

1. Pupil
1 burnt umber +
1 recipe #2

2. Iris Main
3 white + 1 cerulean blue hue + 1 raw sienna + 1 speck Naples yellow hue

3. Iris Medium
3 white + 1 cerulean blue hue + 1 speck Naples yellow hue

4. Iris Light
2 white + 1 recipe #3 + 1 speck cadmium yellow light

5. Iris Highlight
2 white +
1 speck Naples yellow hue

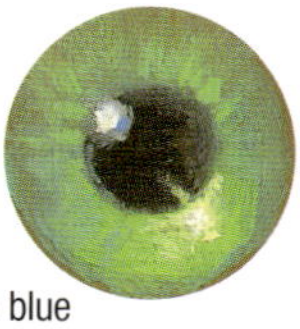

MAIN COLOR BLENDS

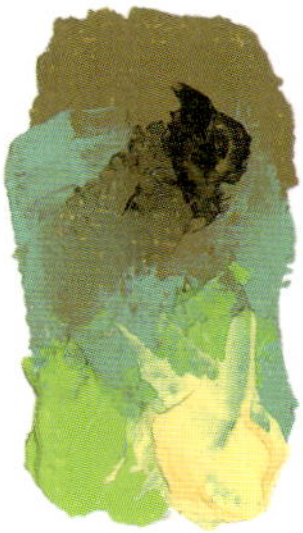

HAZEL

Hazel eyes can be warm, cool, or slightly gray in color. Manipulate these basic mixes with cadmium orange to warm; viridian green to cool; and a warm purple mix to gray.

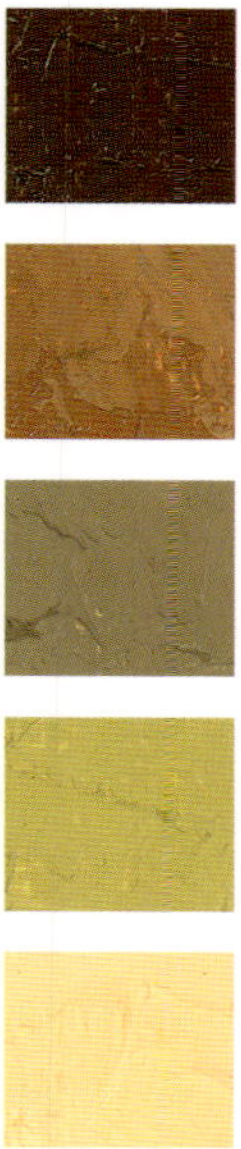

1. Pupil
1 burnt umber +
1 raw sienna

2. Iris Main
1 white +
1 raw sienna

3. Iris Medium
3 white + 1 raw sienna + 1 speck ultramarine blue

4. Iris Light
1 white + 2 Naples yellow hue + 1 speck viridian green

5. Iris Highlight
2 white +
1 speck Naples yellow hue

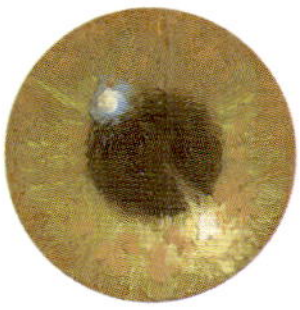

MAIN COLOR BLENDS

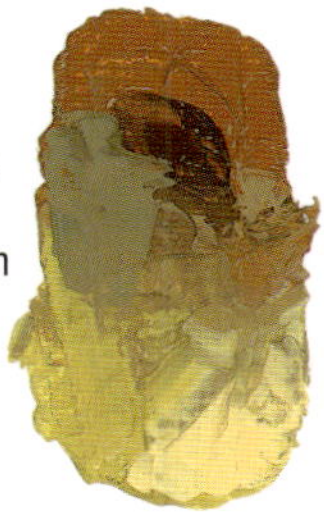

GRAY

Some gray eyes appear to have a cold look, whereas others appear warmer. For a cool, steely look, add a speck of cerulean blue hue and raw umber to the mix. Use ultramarine blue or cobalt blue for a warmer color.

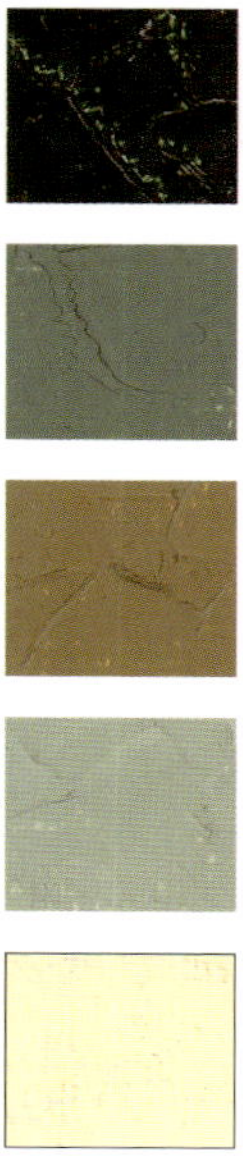

1. Pupil
9 viridian green +
1 cadmium red light

2. Iris Main
1 recipe #1 +
2 white

3. Iris Medium
6 white +
2 recipe #1 +
1 cadmium orange

4. Iris Light
4 white +
1 recipe #1

5. Iris Highlight
2 white + 1 speck Naples yellow hue +
1 speck cadmium orange

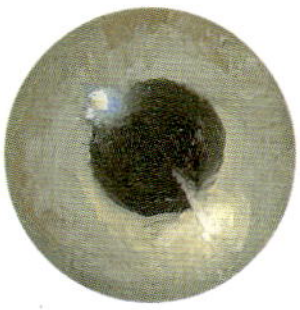

MAIN COLOR BLENDS

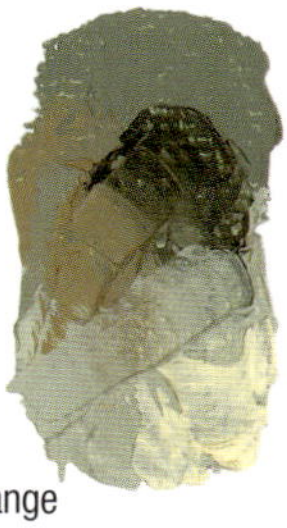

DARK BROWN

Dark brown hair is usually warm in color. If your model has hair that is a bit cooler, add a small speck of viridian green or ultramarine blue to the mix.

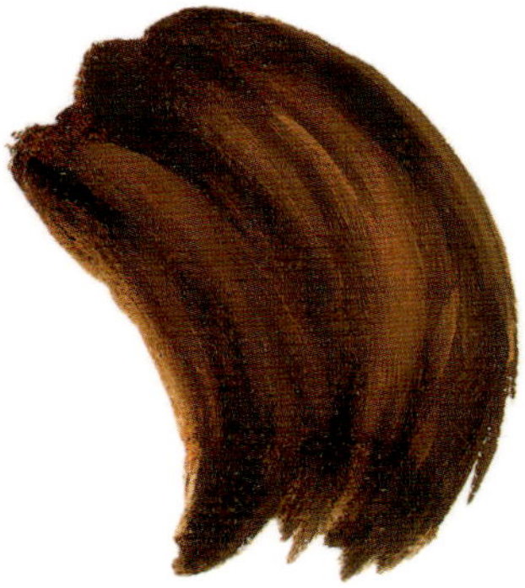

SHADOWS	MAIN COLOR	HIGHLIGHTS

1. 3 burnt umber 2 burnt sienna	**2.** 1 burnt sienna 1 raw sienna	**3.** 1 white 1 raw sienna 1 cadmium orange

BROWN

This is just slightly lighter in value than dark brown, but it is also warm in color. Keep value changes subtle. Do not use pure white as a highlight—instead add white to the light recipe.

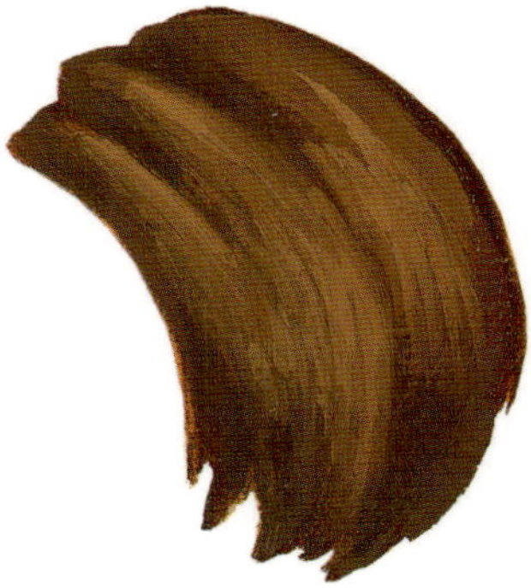

SHADOWS	MAIN COLOR	HIGHLIGHTS

1. 2 burnt sienna 2 burnt umber 1 white	**2.** 1 recipe #1 1 yellow ochre 1 white	**3.** 1 recipe #2 2 white

GOLDEN BROWN

Golden brown is a bit richer in yellow than the two previous browns. Raw sienna is the dominant color in these recipes. Again, don't use only white to lighten; remember to add color as well (see page 6).

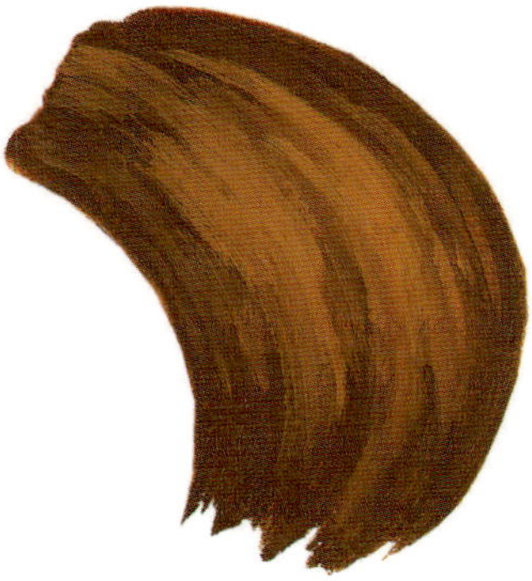

SHADOWS	MAIN COLOR	HIGHLIGHTS
		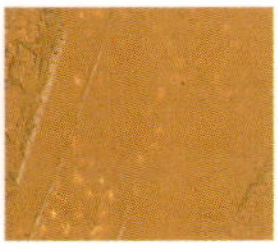
1. 3 raw sienna 2 burnt sienna 1 burnt umber	**2.** 2 raw sienna 1 white	**3.** 6 Naples yellow hue 1 white 1 raw sienna

LIGHT BROWN

The colors in light brown hair can be a bit cooler than those in brown or dark brown. Use a little viridian green or a touch of cerulean blue hue to cool colors, if necessary.

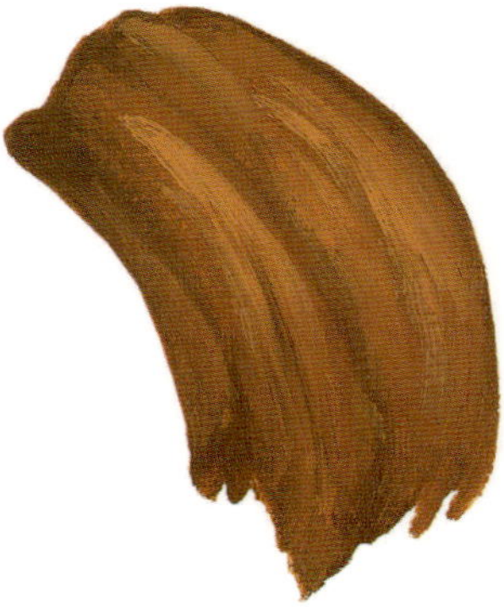

SHADOWS	MAIN COLOR	HIGHLIGHTS
		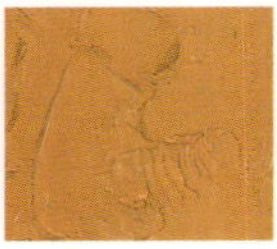
1. 4 raw sienna 1 burnt umber 2 white 2 specks burnt sienna	**2.** 4 yellow ochre 4 Naples yellow hue 1 burnt sienna	**3.** 1 recipe #2 2 white

AUBURN

Auburn hair is very rich in dark reds mingled with deep browns. Notice that this set of recipes includes both a warm red (cadmium red light) and a cool red (alizarin crimson).

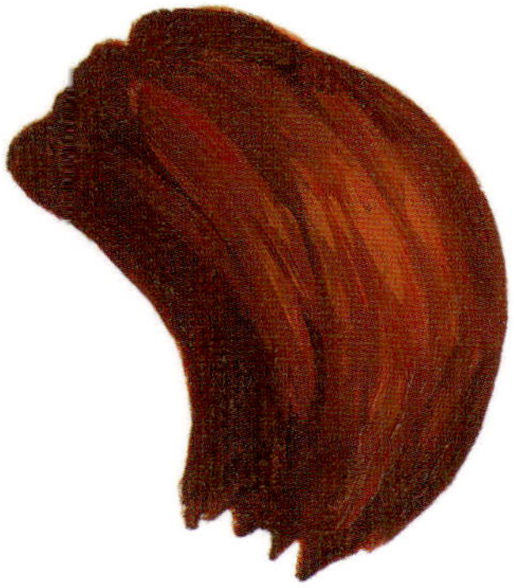

SHADOWS	MAIN COLOR	HIGHLIGHTS

1. 2 alizarin crimson 2 burnt sienna 1 burnt umber	**2.** 1 burnt sienna 1 cadmium red light	**3.** 2 yellow ochre 1 cadmium red light

RED

Reds can range from rich, deep reds to carrotlike orange tones. In these recipes, cool phthalo red tones down the warmth of cadmium orange without losing color intensity.

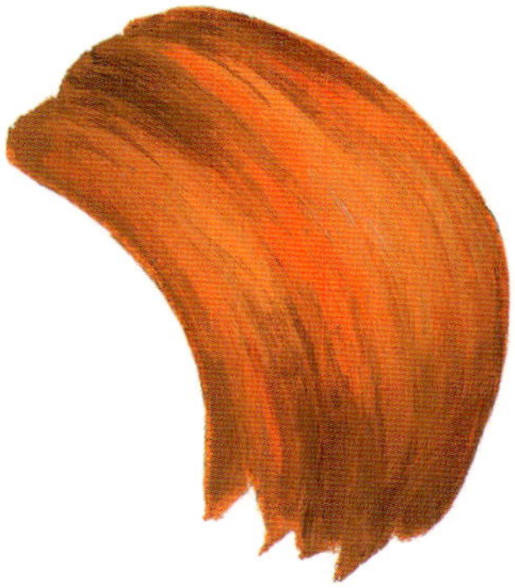

SHADOWS	MAIN COLOR	HIGHLIGHTS

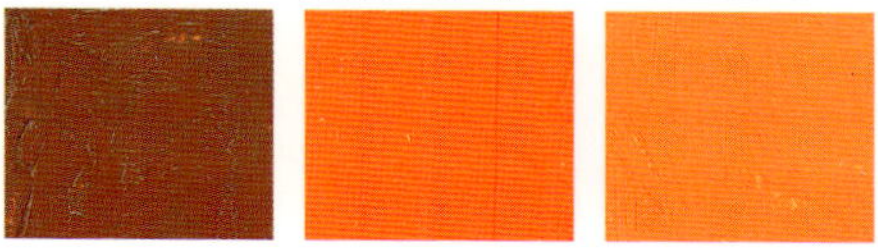

1. 2 raw sienna 1 cadmium orange 1 speck cadmium red light 1 speck burnt umber	**2.** 1 cadmium orange 1 speck phthalo red	**3.** 1 Naples yellow hue 2 specks cadmium orange 1 speck cad. yellow light

STRAWBERRY BLOND

This color can be tricky. Some hair leans toward the reds without being "red," whereas other hair leans toward the orange-tan range of color. Add a speck of cadmium vermilion to these mixes if you need a redder tint.

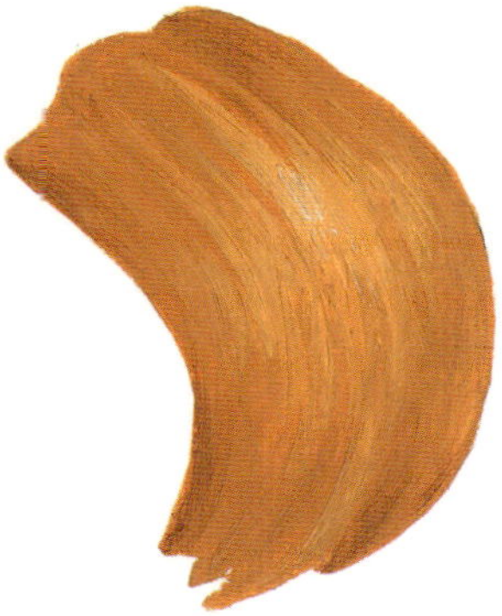

SHADOWS	MAIN COLOR	HIGHLIGHTS

1. 1 raw sienna 1 Naples yellow hue 1 speck cad. red light	**2.** 1 Naples yellow hue 1 speck cad. red light	**3.** 1 recipe #2 2 white

GOLDEN BLOND

The colors in some golden blond hair can be fairly strong. The value is usually lighter than strawberry blond and is a little less red in hue. Use cadmium yellow medium to make these colors appear more golden.

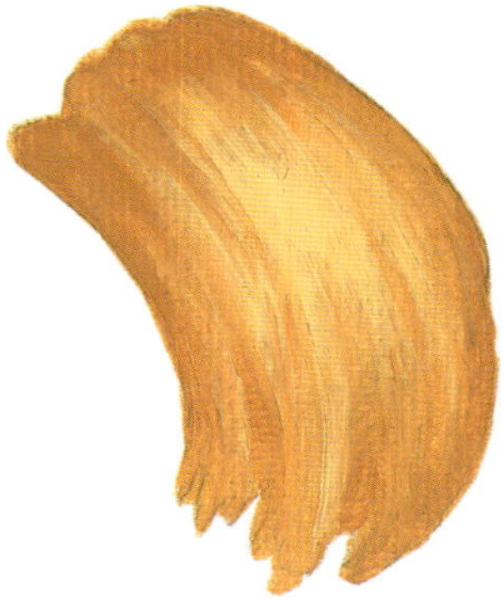

SHADOWS	MAIN COLOR	HIGHLIGHTS

1. 2 Naples yellow hue 1 raw sienna	**2.** 2 Naples yellow hue 1 speck cad. yellow med.	**3.** 6 white 1 cad. yellow med. 1 speck Naples yellow hue

PALE BLOND

Keep the colors fresh by limiting the use of white. Naples yellow hue, cadmium yellow medium, and raw sienna mixed with white make good combinations for this hair color.

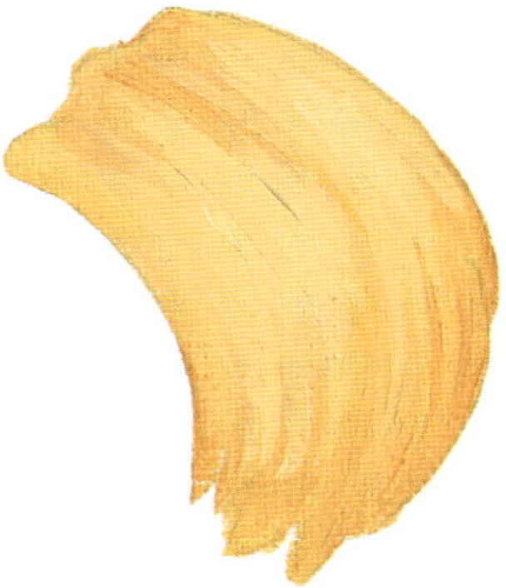

SHADOWS	MAIN COLOR	HIGHLIGHTS
1. 1 white 1 Naples yellow hue 1 raw sienna	**2.** 1 white 1 Naples yellow hue	**3.** 6 white 1 Naples yellow hue 1 speck cad. yellow med.

ASH BLOND

This hair color contains more green than the others do. However, it must be very subtle and used only to affect the other colors in creating the ash appearance.

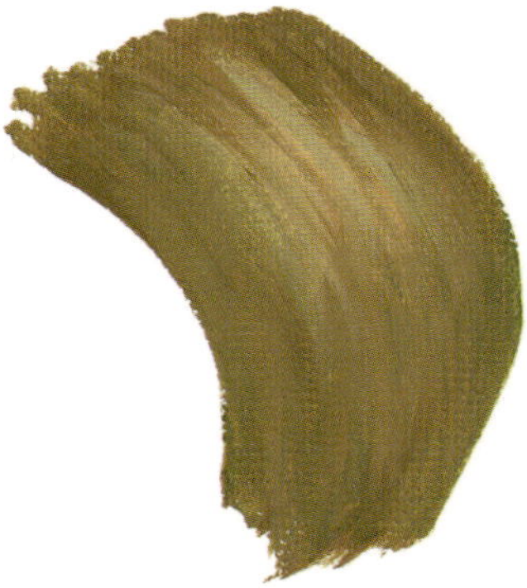

SHADOWS	MAIN COLOR	HIGHLIGHTS
1. 4 white 3 raw sienna 1 chrome oxide green	**2.** 4 white 1 yellow ochre 1 chrome oxide green	**3.** 1 white 1 speck raw sienna 1 speck chrome oxide green

WARM WHITE

When painting white hair, try to keep the colors from appearing chalky. Also limit the use of yellows in white hair, as they can cause the hair to appear heavy and unclean.

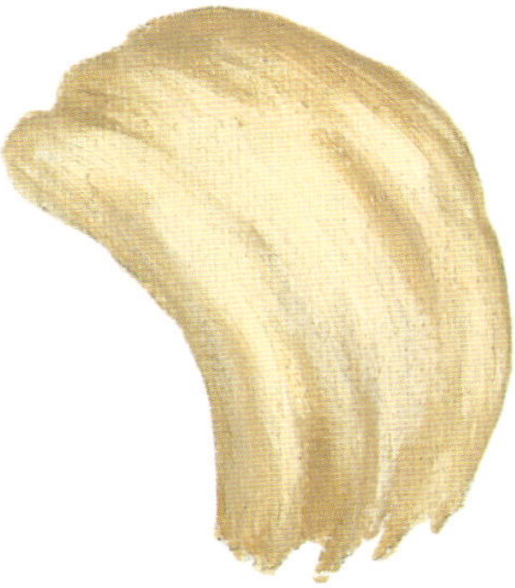

SHADOWS	MAIN COLOR	HIGHLIGHTS
1. 1 white 1 speck burnt umber	**2.** 1 white 1 speck burnt sienna	**3.** 1 white 1 speck cadmium orange

COOL WHITE

Colors in cool white must also be kept to a minimum. Ultramarine blue is a warm blue. It contains a bit of red, making it a purplish-blue that is perfect for cool white hair.

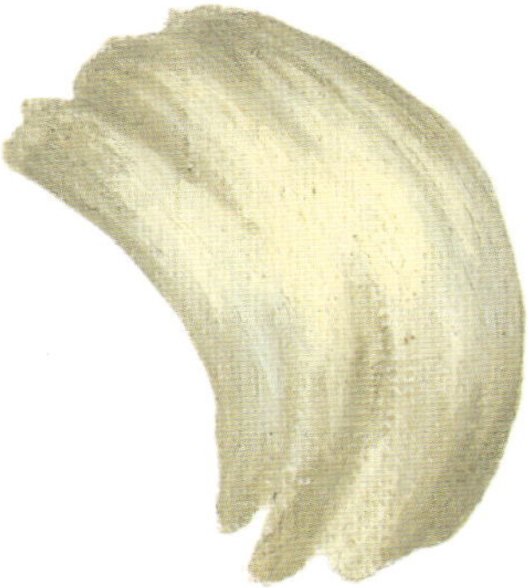

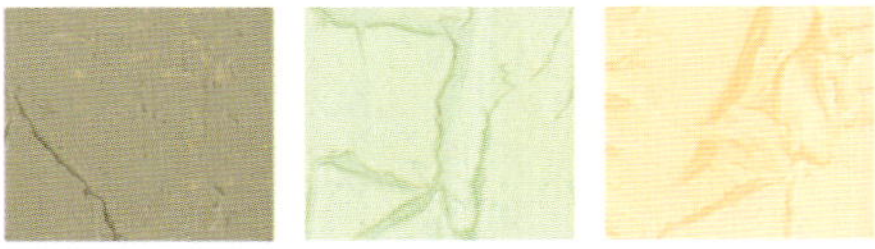

SHADOWS	MAIN COLOR	HIGHLIGHTS
1. 1 white 1 speck burnt umber 1 speck ultramarine blue	**2.** 1 white 1 speck ultramarine blue	**3.** White (pure)

WARM GRAY

Gray hair also contains color. As in white hair, keep the colors soft. If your model has warm gray with more brown-red tones, use burnt umber and a speck of cadmium red light.

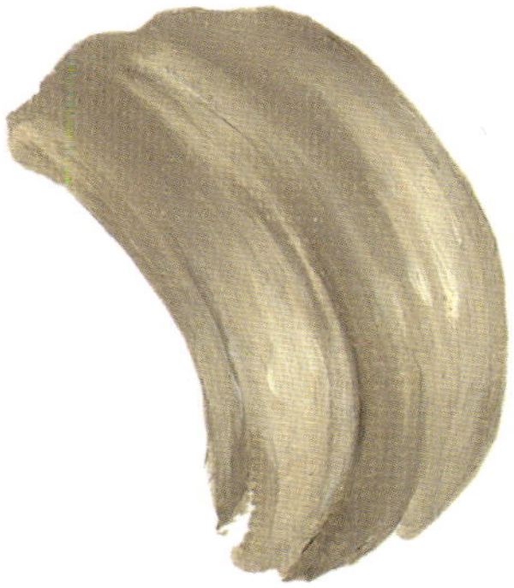

SHADOWS	MAIN COLOR	HIGHLIGHTS

1. 6 white 1 burnt umber 1 ultramarine blue	**2.** 1 white 1 speck burnt umber 1 speck alizarin crimson	**3.** 2 white 1 speck burnt sienna

COOL GRAY

Use ivory black for this hair color. It is a warm black, and it's weaker than other blacks. When mixed with the other recipes here (all of which contain ultramarine blue), it works perfectly.

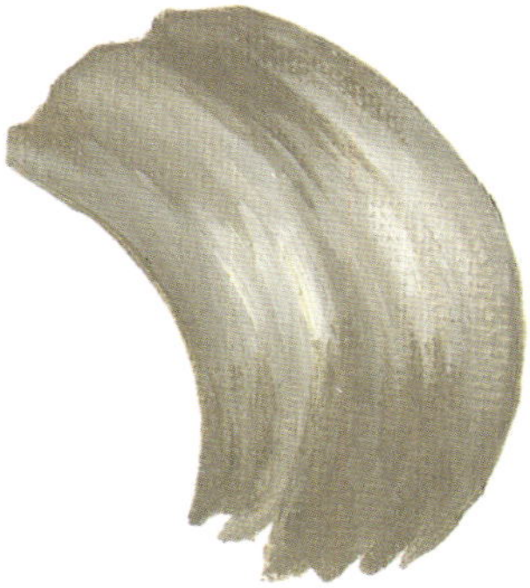

SHADOWS	MAIN COLOR	HIGHLIGHTS

1. 8 white 1 black	**2.** 2 white 1 speck ultramarine blue 1 speck alizarin crimson 1 speck black	**3.** 2 white 1 speck ultramarine blue

WARM BLACK

This hair color contains recipes that reflect warm highlights. Make your own black for the dark recipe with burnt umber and ultramarine blue. This way you can make it cooler with more blue or warmer with more umber.

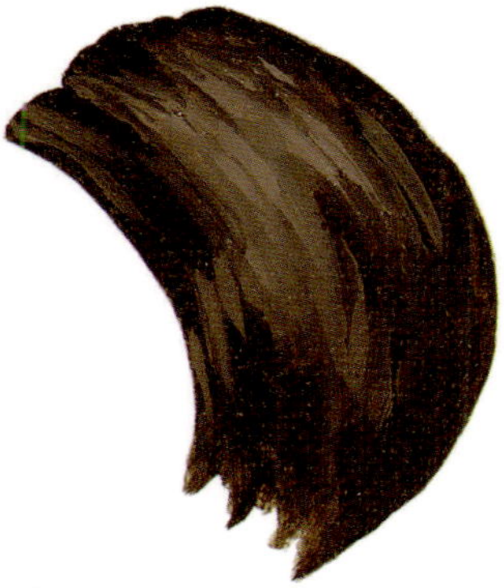

SHADOWS	MAIN COLOR	HIGHLIGHTS

1. 1 burnt umber 1 ultramarine blue	**2.** 1 recipe #1 2 white 3 specks burnt sienna	**3.** 1 recipe #2 2 white 2 specks alizarin crimson

COOL BLACK

For cool black, use a mix of black and ultramarine blue. The addition of ultramarine blue along with alizarin crimson in the light recipe gives the color a slight purplish tone.

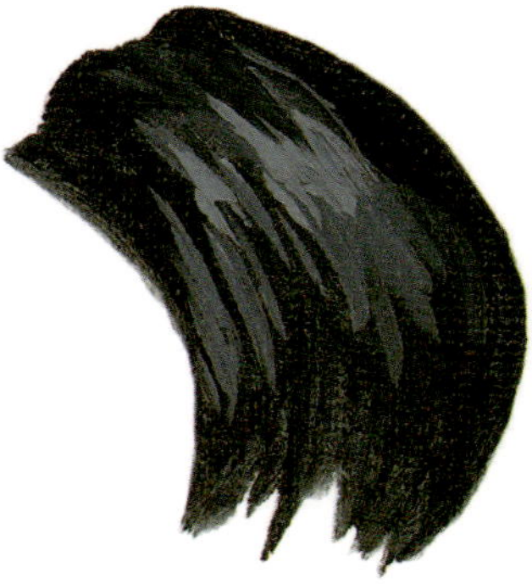

SHADOWS	MAIN COLOR	HIGHLIGHTS

1. 1 black 1 ultramarine blue	**2.** 1 recipe #1 1 white	**3.** 1 recipe #2 1 white 1 speck alizarin crimson

SkinToneRecipes

WATERCOLOR COLORS USED

- Burnt Umber
- Burnt Sienna
- Cadmium Red Light
- Hooker's Green Deep
- Permanent Rose
- Ultramarine Blue
- Yellow Ochre

Mix until the color matches the **Master Skin Tone Recipe** shown at right.

1. 50% yellow ochre
50% cadmium red light
Water: level 5

1. MASTER SKIN TONE RECIPE

COLOR/WATER LEVELS

Level 1 Pale Color

Level 2 Weak Color

Level 3 Medium Color

Level 4 Strong Color

Level 5 Very Strong Color

LIGHT VALUES

2. 100% master recipe
Water: level 1

3. 100% master recipe
Water: level 2

4. 95% master recipe
5% recipe #11
Water: level 2

MIDDLE VALUES

5. 80% master recipe
20% recipe #12
Water: level 3

6. 70% master recipe
30% recipe #12
Water: level 3

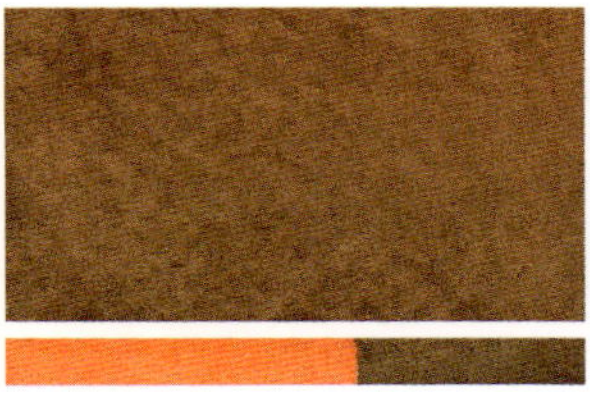

7. 60% master recipe
40% recipe #13
Water: level 4

DARK/GRAYED VALUES

8. 80% master recipe
20% recipe #14
Water: level 3

9. 60% master recipe
25% recipe #14
15% recipe #12
Water: level 4

10. 60% master recipe
30% recipe #13
10% ultramarine blue
Water: level 4

HIGHLIGHT VALUE

11. 1 speck permanent rose
Water: level 1

WARM SHADOW

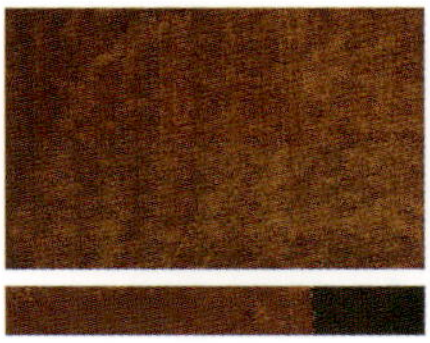

12. 75% burnt sienna
25% burnt umber
Water: level 4

COOL SHADOW

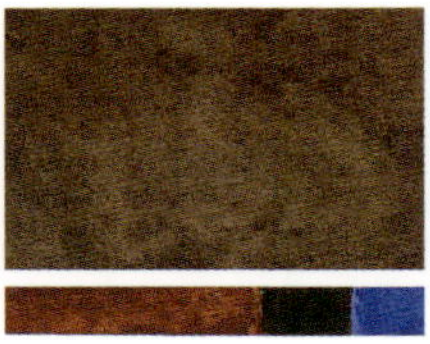

13. 60% burnt sienna
20% burnt umber
20% ultramarine blue
Water: level 4

GRAYING COLOR

14. 100% Hooker's green deep
Water: level 4

Skin Tone Recipes

WATERCOLOR COLORS USED

- Burnt Sienna
- Burnt Umber
- Cadmium Red Light
- Cerulean Blue Hue
- Cobalt Blue
- Permanent Rose
- Raw Sienna
- Sepia
- Viridian Green

Mix until the color matches the **Master Skin Tone Recipe** shown at right.

1. 85% raw sienna
15% cerulean blue hue
Water: level 5

1. MASTER SKIN TONE RECIPE

COLOR/WATER LEVELS

Level 1 Pale Color

Level 2 Weak Color

Level 3 Medium Color

Level 4 Strong Color

Level 5 Very Strong Color

LIGHT VALUES

2. 95% master recipe
5% cadmium red light
Water: level 2

3. 90% master recipe
10% cadmium red light
Water: level 3

4. 80% master recipe
20% burnt sienna
Water: level 3

MIDDLE VALUES

5. 60% master recipe
40% burnt umber
Water: level 3

6. 85% master recipe
15% viridian green
Water: level 3

7. 60% master recipe
40% recipe #14
Water: level 3

DARK/GRAYED VALUES

8. 45% master recipe
45% recipe #12
10% permanent rose
Water: level 3

9. 40% burnt sienna
40% recipe #14
20% master recipe
Water: level 4

10. 50% master recipe
50% recipe #12
Water: level 4

HIGHLIGHT VALUE

11. 1 speck any color above
Water: level 1

WARM SHADOW

12. 100% sepia
Water: level 3

COOL SHADOW

13. 50% sepia
50% viridian green
Water: level 3

GRAYING COLOR

14. 80% cobalt blue
20% master recipe
Water: level 3

SkinToneRecipes

WATERCOLOR COLORS USED

- Burnt Sienna
- Burnt Umber
- Cadmium Orange
- Cerulean Blue Hue
- Cobalt Blue
- Permanent Rose
- Viridian Green
- Yellow Ochre

Mix until the color matches the **Master Skin Tone Recipe** shown at right.

1. 60% yellow ochre
30% cadmium orange
10% permanent rose
Water: level 5

1. MASTER SKIN TONE RECIPE

COLOR/WATER LEVELS

Level 1 Pale Color
Level 2 Weak Color
Level 3 Medium Color
Level 4 Strong Color
Level 5 Very Strong Color

LIGHT VALUES

2. 100% master recipe
Water: level 1

3. 100% master recipe
Water: level 2

4. 100% master recipe
Water: level 2.5

MIDDLE VALUES

5. 100% master recipe
Water: level 3

6. 70% master recipe
30% burnt sienna
Water: level 3

7. 70% master recipe
30% burnt umber
Water: level 3

DARK/GRAYED VALUES

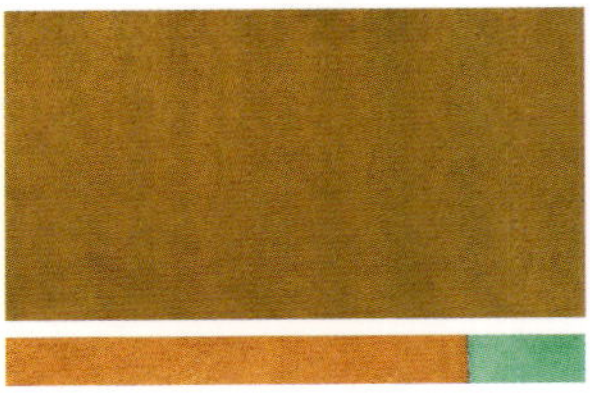

8. 80% master recipe
20% recipe #14
Water: level 4

9. 70% master recipe
30% recipe #12
Water: level 4

10. 75% recipe #13
25% master recipe
Water: level 4

HIGHLIGHT VALUE

11. 1 speck any color above
Water: level 1

WARM SHADOW

12. 90% burnt sienna
10% cobalt blue
Water: level 4

COOL SHADOW

13. 90% burnt umber
10% cobalt blue
Water: level 4

GRAYING COLOR

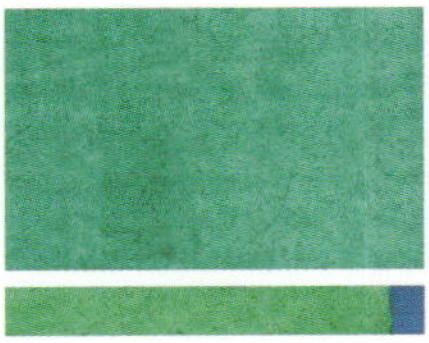

14. 95% viridian green
5% cerulean blue hue
Water: level 4

WATERCOLOR COLORS USED

- Alizarin Crimson
- Burnt Sienna
- Burnt Umber
- Cadmium Orange
- Cobalt Blue
- Permanent Rose
- Raw Sienna

Mix until the color matches the **Master Skin Tone Recipe** shown at right.

1. 40% raw sienna
40% cadmium orange
20% burnt umber
Water: level 5

1. MASTER SKIN TONE RECIPE

COLOR / WATER LEVELS

Level 1 Pale Color
Level 2 Weak Color
Level 3 Medium Color
Level 4 Strong Color
Level 5 Very Strong Color

LIGHT VALUES

2. 100% master recipe
Water: level 1

3. 97% master recipe
3% permanent rose
Water: level 2

4. 95% master recipe
5% permanent rose
Water: level 3

MIDDLE VALUES

5. 90% master recipe
10% burnt sienna
Water: level 3

6. 85% master recipe
10% burnt sienna
5% alizarin crimson
Water: level 4

7. 70% master recipe
20% burnt umber
10% alizarin crimson
Water: level 4

DARK/GRAYED VALUES

8. 75% recipe #12
25% master recipe
Water: level 4

9. 75% recipe #13
25% master recipe
Water: level 4

10. 80% recipe #14
20% master recipe
Water: level 4

HIGHLIGHT VALUE

11. 1 speck cadmium orange
Water: level 1

WARM SHADOW

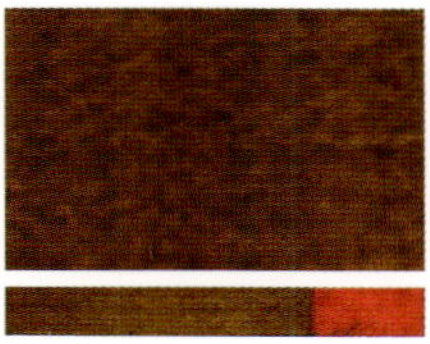

12. 75% burnt umber
25% alizarin crimson
Water: level 4

COOL SHADOW

13. 60% burnt umber
40% cobalt blue
Water: level 4

GRAYING COLOR

14. 70% cobalt blue
30% alizarin crimson
Water: level 3

SkinToneRecipes

WATERCOLOR COLORS USED

- Burnt Sienna
- Burnt Umber
- Cerulean Blue Hue
- Ivory Black
- Lemon Yellow
- Permanent Rose
- Sap Green

Mix until the color matches the **Master Skin Tone Recipe** shown at right.

1. 60% permanent rose
40% lemon yellow
Water: level 5

1. MASTER SKIN TONE RECIPE

COLOR / WATER LEVELS

Level 1 Pale Color

Level 2 Weak Color

Level 3 Medium Color

Level 4 Strong Color

Level 5 Very Strong Color

LIGHT VALUES

2. 90% master recipe
10% lemon yellow
Water: level 1

3. 100% master recipe
Water: level 1.5

4. 100% master recipe
Water: level 2

MIDDLE VALUES

5. 95% master recipe
5% permanent rose
Water: level 3

6. 50% recipe #12
50% master recipe
Water: level 3

7. 70% master recipe
30% recipe #13
Water: level 3

DARK / GRAYED VALUES

8. 50% master recipe
50% recipe #14
Water: level 3.5

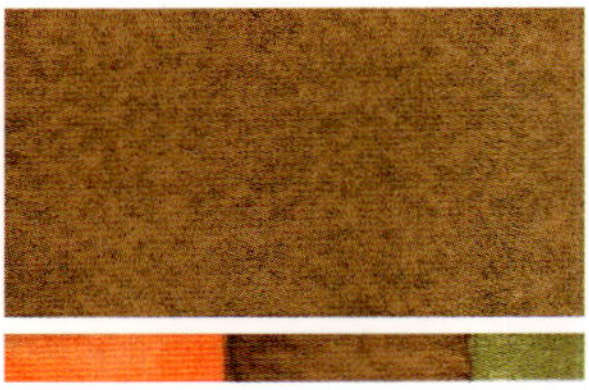

9. 40% master recipe
40% burnt umber
20% recipe #14
Water: level 4

10. 90% master recipe
10% cerulean blue hue
Water: level 4

HIGHLIGHT VALUE

11. 1 speck lemon yellow
Water: level 1

WARM SHADOW

12. 90% burnt sienna
10% master recipe
Water: level 3

COOL SHADOW

13. 70% master recipe
30% black
Water: level 4

GRAYING COLOR

14. 60% master recipe
40% sap green
Water: level 3

Skin Tone Recipes

WATERCOLOR COLORS USED

- Burnt Sienna
- Burnt Umber
- Cadmium Red Light
- Lemon Yellow
- New Gamboge
- Viridian Green

Mix until the color matches the **Master Skin Tone Mix** shown at right.

1. 60% cadmium red light
40% new gamboge
Water: level 5

1. MASTER SKIN TONE RECIPE

COLOR / WATER LEVELS

Level 1 Pale Color
Level 2 Weak Color
Level 3 Medium Color
Level 4 Strong Color
Level 5 Very Strong Color

LIGHT VALUES

2. 100% master recipe
Water: level 1

3. 100% master recipe
Water: level 2

4. 90% master recipe
10% lemon yellow
Water: level 2

MIDDLE VALUES

5. 90% master recipe
10% new gamboge
Water: level 3

6. 95% master recipe
5% new gamboge
Water: level 3

7. 100% master recipe
Water: level 3.5

DARK/GRAYED VALUES

8. 50% master recipe
50% recipe #12
Water: level 3

9. 50% master recipe
50% recipe #13
Water: level 3

10. 65% master recipe
35% recipe #14
Water: level 3

HIGHLIGHT VALUE

11. 1 speck any color above
Water: level 1

WARM SHADOW

12. 50% burnt sienna
50% burnt umber
Water: level 3

COOL SHADOW

13. 100% burnt umber
Water: level 4

GRAYING COLOR

14. 100% viridian green
Water: level 3

You can create your own master recipes for a completely new variation of skin tones. Use the examples here and create your own combinations. You can even create your own original master recipes. By adding additional colors to the selected master recipe, the combinations are endless.

1. Page 21 Master Recipe

3. New Master Recipe

2. Page 15 Master Recipe

5. Recipe #4 warmed with white and Naples yellow hue

4. Recipe #3 lightened with white

6. Recipe #4 grayed with viridian green

By selecting master recipes that are very different in tone, you can achieve almost any color. You can even lighten, darken, warm, cool, or gray the recipes. Mixing Page 15's Master Recipe with Page 28's Master Recipe creates some beautiful skin tones. Vary the mix amounts for even a wider range of skin tone colors.

1. Page 15 Master Recipe

3. New Master Recipe

2. Page 28 Master Recipe

5. Recipe #4 warmed with white and Naples yellow hue

4. Recipe #3 lightened with white

6. Recipe #4 grayed with viridian green

Like the master recipes, subsequent value recipes also can be altered. They can be intermixed (creating a new color), lightened, darkened, grayed, and so on. This first example is golden tones mixed with ruddy tones. This creates a new and beautiful color mix. Add more of the ruddy tones for a redder color.

1. Page 22 Recipe #3 | **3. New Skin Tone Recipe** | **2. Page 18 Recipe #5**

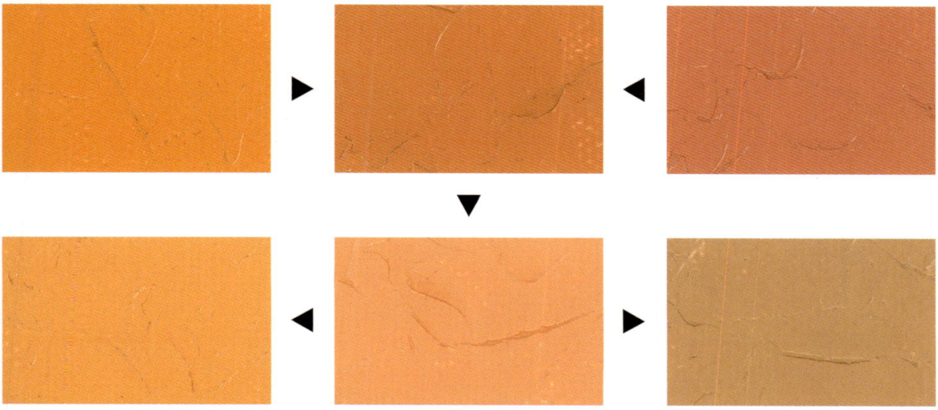

5. Recipe #4 warmed with white and cadmium yellow light | **4. Recipe #3 lightened with white** | **6. Recipe #4 grayed with cerulean blue hue**

You will notice similarities in the recipes. However, there are slight tonal differences that are extremely important in matching a model's skin tone. You can also add raw colors to these recipes. For instance, if your model is reddish in tone, find and add the correct red, warm, cool, dark, light, and so on.

1. Page 20 Recipe #4 | **3. New Skin Tone Recipe** | **2. Page 19 Recipe #7**

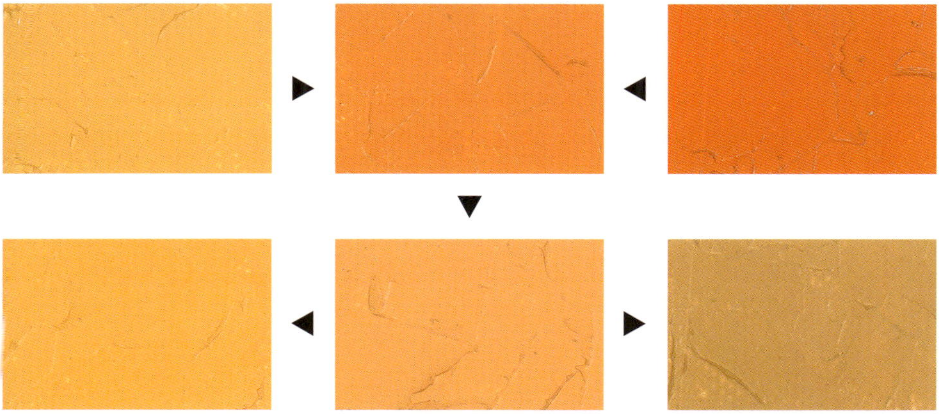

5. Recipe #4 warmed with white and zinc yellow | **4. Recipe #3 lightened with white** | **6. Recipe #4 grayed with chrome oxide green**

Index

Oil/Acrylic Conversion **Chart**

OIL COLOR NAME	ACRYLIC COLOR NAME	EQUIVALENT MIXTURE
Alizarin crimson	Alizarin crimson	
Burnt sienna	Burnt sienna	
Burnt umber	Burnt umber	
Cadmium orange	Cadmium orange	
Cadmium red light	Cadmium red light	
Cadmium vermilion	Vermilion hue *(or use mixture)*	**1 part Indo orange-red + 1 speck Naphthol crimson**
Cadmium yellow light	Cadmium yellow light	
Cadmium yellow medium	Cadmium yellow medium	
Cerulean blue hue	*not available (use mixture)*	**1 cerulean blue + 1 speck phthalo blue**
Chrome oxide green	Chromium oxide green	
Cobalt blue	Cobalt blue	
Ivory black	Ivory black	
Naples yellow hue	Naples yellow hue permanent *(or use mixture)*	**4 parts yellow ochre/oxide + 1 part white + 2 specks cadmium orange**
Phthalo red	Naphthol crimson or phthalo crimson	
Raw sienna	Raw sienna	
Raw umber	Raw umber	
Titanium white	Titanium white	
Ultramarine blue	Ultramarine blue	
Venetian red	Venetian red or red oxide	
Viridian green	Viridian green or viridian hue permanent	
Yellow ochre	Yellow ochre or yellow oxide	
Zinc yellow	Yellow light hansa	

About the Author

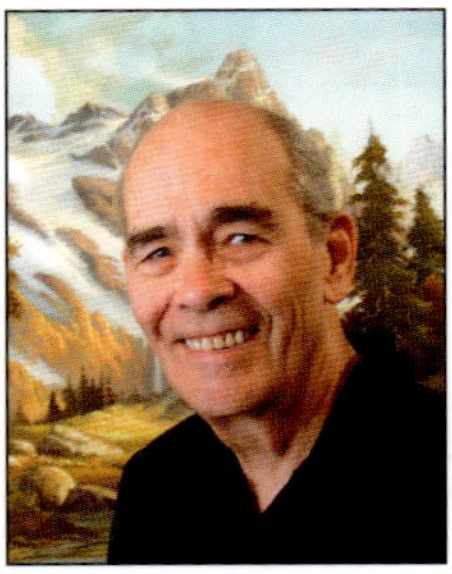

William F. Powell is an internationally recognized artist and one of America's foremost colorists. A native of Huntington, West Virginia, Bill studied at the Art Student's Career School in New York; Harrow Technical College in Harrow England; and the Louvre Free School of Art in Paris France. He has been professionally involved in fine art, commercial art, and technical illustrations for more than 45 years. His experience as an art instructor includes oil, watercolor, acrylic, colored pencil and pastel—with subjects ranging from landscapes to portraits and wildlife. He has also authored a number of art instruction books including several popular Walter Foster titles. As a renowned master of color, Bill has conducted numerous "Color Mixing and Theory" workshops in various cities throughout the U.S. His expertise in color theory also led him to author and illustrate several articles and an educational series of 11 articles entitled "Color in Perspective" for a national art magazine. Additionally he has performed as an art consultant for national space programs and for several artist's paint manufacturers. Bill's work has also included the creation of background sets for films, model making, animated cartoons, and animated films for computer mockup programs. He also produces instructional painting, color mixing, and drawing art videos.

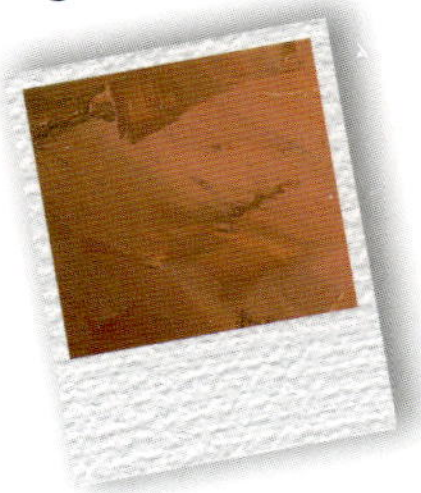